"The saying "life doesn't come with a handbook" never knew Christina. It's not that she has all the answers, she's just damn good at asking the right questions at the right time. After a successful career, raising a family, several house renovations, two marriages and one rescue dog, I came to a crossroads as my career evolved, my children moved out and my marriage and dog settled into "middle age." I was restless. Enter Christina and her persistent questions. It's not that life wasn't good, it's that, to quote her—"I knew I was meant for more."

The idea that the answers were inside me, they just needed to be vetted, and organized and I needed to be held accountable for finding them felt like what previously had seemed unachievable might really be possible. Through a series of exercises and tools, some of which are inside this book, I felt supported, challenged, and motivated to shift from what "might be" to what was. Christina gave me the tools and the courage to use them to start my next chapter. I'm so glad she is sharing them inside the pages of this book."

—**JULIE GROVES,** *Artist, and former Chief Executive Officer*

———

"Working with Christina has been truly transformative—both personally and professionally. Before working with Christina, I was mired down by imposter syndrome as well as the classic middle child syndrome. I constantly questioned if I deserved to be at the table if I was good enough if I was worthy of being on the stage I was on, or if was I just "lucky?" I had trouble believing in myself, seeing my accomplishments as my own, and voicing my thoughts and opinions confidently. I didn't believe in myself.

Christina changed all of that and I will be forever grateful to her—for not only seeing the best in me and believing in me but for also allowing me to finally see the best in myself and to believe in myself and my abilities. I have learned so much from this incredibly inspiring, kindhearted, strong, badass woman— I listen with more intent, I have found my voice, I communicate with those around me clearly and thoughtfully, and most of all, I see my superpowers and I finally see and feel my purpose.

She not only brings me my Sunday Sunshine, but she has also lit a fire within me that shines brightly. I know this book will help you find your superpowers and feel that renewed purpose."

—**KOMEL CARUSO**, *Chief Growth Office, HerMD*

———

"To those looking for clarity and direction, Christina Langdon is that rarest of gifts. She has the kind of in-the-trenches business and leadership experience to understand your position fully—and the human perspective and life experience to offer real advice and action. Where other advisors and coaches share platitudes or rigid business dogma, Christina tells you the truth and then helps you live it. Her Sunday blog posts are a must read for me—even after 25 years of being a coach and trainer myself. This book needs to be on your night table—and mine!"

—**DOUG WEAVER**, *C.E.O., Upstream Group and Author of* The Drift

———

"On my very first working day at Martha Stewart, I was excited, scared, and intimidated. Christina graciously extended her support, kindness, brilliant sense of humor, and authentic self to me. It wasn't just me—her encouragement of others, her energy, vulnerability, original perspective, joyful laughter, and honest soul showed up every day—prepared to "ride the waves" and help us all be the best we could be, as individuals and as a team. It is rare to find someone so committed and yet so selfless. Christina has both long-term and short-term goals, a fantastic business skill that few leaders really understand.

Instead of letting the personal difficulties and challenges Christina has faced distract or derail her, they fueled a resilient attitude and strength of character and purpose like no one I have ever known. It has been on her most difficult days that Christina has found the courage to help and inspire others—never dwelling on "why me", knowing that her power would come from pulling others through *their* bumpy days. In her own Sunday Sunshine words, "be the person that handles hard better"!

—**SALLY PRESTON**, *Chief Revenue Officer, The Effie's*

———————

"Being a founder can sometimes be the loneliest job in the whole world. There are days filled with self-doubt, angst, hurdles, fires, and tears. Other days are filled with laughter, triumph, and success. As a founder, the goal is to string as many great days together as possible and not waste time trying to put out fires. Christina's book is filled with sound advice, and wisdom and is like a trusted friend helping you navigate the precarious founder journey. Christina helps quiet the negative voices and empowers the dreamer within to take the stage that you deserve and to reach your fullest potential."

—**DR. SOMI JAVAID**, *Founder & Chief Medical Officer, HerMD*

FOR SUCCESS SAKE!

Simple Steps for
Extraordinary Possibilities
in Leadership and Life

Christina Langdon
Business Growth Strategist and Leadership Coach

CHRISTINA
LANGDON
high performance coaching + consulting

Book Editor: Lori Sussle Bonanni
Design by Katie Flanagan

"The most influential person in your life is you, and when you recognize your influence over you, it's a game changer."

-*Christina Langdon*

Contents

*Success is not waiting
out there. It's an inside
job waiting for you.*

Preface

A VISION FOR MY EXTRAORDINARY LIFE AND YOURS

My sabbatical came not by a vacation or an educational pursuit but with the diagnosis of AML Leukemia on April Fools' Day 2019 — of all the days.

The next day I would begin the year-long journey through treatment that included 35 consecutive days in the hospital, four additional outpatient rounds, and another 25 nights in the hospital to treat side effects.

Before my diagnosis, I'd successfully conquered single motherhood and launched three exceptional children: Caroline, Jack, and Teddy. I was happily remarried and, by all accounts, successful and content. My resume reflected my career trajectory working for big-name media brands, including Martha Stewart Omnimedia and Fast Company.

After I was 'exiled' from Fast Company, my husband and I became entrepreneurs and opened up a local business which was new, exciting, and something we were building together. Still, there was a constant whisper inside me running on a loop, "You are meant for more."

I felt unfulfilled without an internal compass. I was shouldering disappointment that I should have achieved more of an impact in the media business and was comparing myself to others who had the smarts, longevity, and ability to handle it all.

My unmet expectations, and an unclear definition of my success, had me feeling trapped. Rumblings of anxiety filled with discontent and panic bubbled just beneath the surface every day. My "should have, would have, could have" mindset was debilitating and destructive. This was not the life I wanted.

Intellectually, I knew the only person who could change my circumstance was me. I was the owner of my destiny but why wasn't I taking ownership? I scolded myself, "Wake the f**k up," "Stop playing the victim," "Stop feeling so sorry for yourself." Nothing seemed to work.

———

Enter my doctor with life-changing words.

"Christina, this is more serious
than we originally thought."

———

Getting diagnosed with cancer was one of the worst possible things I could have ever imagined. Would I lose my hair? Would my children be left without a Mom. Why me?

But a funny thing happened in that moment of crisis.

I had no choice but to slow down from the high-achieving and unhappy treadmill. Spending nearly five weeks in the hospital, and a year at home away from people carrying germs, granted me a unique opportunity to stop complaining about my career, mistakes, and misfortunes. It gave me time to think about what I had accomplished and what I could do with my accomplishments that would be meaningful and have an impact.

The outpouring of support was overwhelming. My family and close friends made sure my every last need was taken care of including, but not limited to, clarity on my treatment when my brain couldn't understand, the expensive and premium mattress pad for my hospital bed, the UGG slippers to keep my feet warm, and the bags of Doritos when I had an appetite.

I was so grateful for all the cards, prayers, gifts, meals, and rides to treatment from close friends and friends that I had not kept in touch with. I was so thankful for all of it, but I was most grateful for the time I now had to reframe what it meant to be here.

That outpouring of love during this time was transformative. Their words of support awakened me.

YOU are...
Strong
Special
Awesome
Tough
Loved
Not alone
Supported
Amazing
Courageous

A fighter
BRAVE!!!!

A friend had handwritten these loving words on the left-hand side of a get-well card.

Were those words really about me? At first, I thought they were kind words coming from sympathy, but slowly, I began to hear them. Hearing kind words about myself that I never allowed myself to believe before. I now wear them on my heart, like the number on an athletic jersey.

With cancer came clarity.

I began to do the work on myself in pursuit of defining what I wanted over what I'd already accomplished so that I would no longer need outside validation. I 'got decided' to become the person I wanted to be. I did the work and started creating the extraordinary life I wanted to live.

Today, I no longer get stuck in the debilitating cycle of self-doubt. My mind was previously laced with fearful thoughts of all kinds like catastrophizing even the smallest of risks. When you have the big 'C' of cancer, your relationship with catastrophe changes.

———

If you only read one thing in this book, read this:

Don't wait for a cancer diagnosis or another
health crisis to become the best version of yourself
or to create what you want for your life.

———

I now understand who the person is that I've been all of my life. I'm still learning how to become the next best version of myself.

Before the diagnosis, I was not yet ready to own my story. I wasn't confident enough to reach out and grab what was mine. This crisis was brought about by my own choices.

I'm now making new choices. I'm on a mission to help others gain clarity and decide on the choices they want to make to achieve their extraordinary life.

In 2020, I launched my coaching and consulting business, where I help Founders and C.E.O.s scale their businesses with more ease and joy. That year of treatment gave me time to get certified in leadership development, coaching, and emotional intelligence.

My love for personal and professional development was born out of working in media, where industry dynamics are full of crisis and change. Leadership coaching has been the red thread throughout my career. I joke that during many lunch hours early in my career, one could find me four blocks from my office in the self-help and leadership aisle at Barnes & Noble.

I own my story and have big, bold plans. I have set a vision for living an extraordinary life that is a work in progress every day. Truth be told, what I do feels so much more than a job. It's become my calling. There's an ease that I live and breathe each day. It's hard work, but my days are finally more joyful.

For Success Sake! is a curated collection of my Sunday Sunshine weekly newsletters, which I started as a means to inspire my clients to think about the week ahead with fresh eyes about what they can create for themselves and their business. You can subscribe at *christinalangdon.com/subscribe.*

You may have heard the term 'Sunday Scaries,' a coined phrase for the anxiety that hits just before the work week begins. Sunday Sunshine seemed like a possible antidote. The response and feedback I have received from clients, colleagues, and friends inspired me to publish this collection of weekly writings.

This book is for anyone who has an itch for more. This book is for the reader ready to get decided—prepared to permit themselves to get sh*t done in their life, career, and/or business. Those who need a nudge to start their next life chapter. It's for anyone who wants to start speaking better to themselves. This book is for those who wish to do tactical exercises to help them gain clarity, get driven, and define what success means. Sprinkled throughout are links to additional resources to help you move from reading about it to creating your extraordinary life.

I'm only an expert in one thing, and that is me. I'm sharing my point of view from thirty years of experience on what has worked for me, my teams, and my clients. In the following pages, I offer perspectives, ideas, practices, exercises, and inspiration to inspire you to do the work to create what you want.

My clients have taught me so much. I have watched them do the work to achieve what they want and to create massive results for themselves and their businesses. Their courageousness is inspiring.

I've been inspired by countless people, and I did my best to acknowledge those who have influenced me throughout this book. On the following pages, you will find the blueprint of what worked for me to reinvent and recreate myself, my business, and my mindset. I hope it will inspire you to achieve success that only you can define.

Success is not waiting out there. It's inside, ready, and waiting for you to get started. Successful people don't wait for their big break; they go and create it.

When I decided to recognize my influence over me, I gave myself permission to achieve success that only I can define. It was game-changing. I am the same person at my core, now with an expanded mind and life-giving willpower. I'm filled with desires and know that they are achieved with hard work and discipline, and by remaining open to possibilities.

I am no different from you.

From the bottom of my heart, thank you for reading.

Here's to living your extraordinary life. It's waiting for you to create it.

BEGINNING

Success, Happiness and Significance

My work is focused on supporting high-performing achievers and visionary leaders in their quests for success, impact, and happiness. I've learned that many people are successful yet remain unhappy.

Success has many definitions — careers, money, and many other things. But things will not bring you happiness.

John Maxwell, author and leadership guru, says happiness is driven not by success but by significance. Significance is how you show up to create, do for others, have an impact, and leave a legacy.

What makes you significant is your ability to access your power, strengths, and unique talents and express them in a way that benefits and impacts the people around you.

Read these sentences for examples of what success looks like as compared to significance.

- A *successful* leader leads.
- A *successful* physician heals.
- A *successful* executive does exceptional work.

- A *significant* leader inspires others to lean into their greatness.
- A *significant* physician heals with empathy to mitigate the fear.
- A *significant* executive does exceptional work and teaches others to do the same.

If you consider yourself successful yet still unhappy, ask yourself, "What is significant about how I show up each day?"

Think about the legacy you want to leave. Legacy sounds big, I know, so simplify it by thinking about what you want to be known for. Then start showing up as that person every day.

———

Your significance is a
building block of your legacy.

———

Likely when you are clear on your significance and have more clarity around how you want to show up with it, you will feel successful.

When you stop being a servant in the life you are living by default and become the creator of the one you want, you will be unstoppable.

Five Truths:

1. Job titles don't make an impact; the people behind them do.
2. Career paths in the right direction are 'right' only if you are happy, growing, and in service to others.
3. You are so much more than the words on your resume.
4. Where you are going is not set by the past but by the future you create.
5. You are the most influential person in your life, and when you recognize your influence over you, it's a game changer.

The C.E.O. of Me

Too often, we default to our shortcomings.

We think about how we fell short and how we could have done it better. We think we should be further ahead or have done things differently. We replay the moment something went wrong and fixate on what we should have done to avoid it.

We focus on what's not working.

How about a daily practice of celebrating ourselves instead of disproportionately focusing on our imagined shortcomings?

To get to where you are today, you've achieved a lot. When was the last time, outside of writing your resume or your bio, you listed all the things you've done, created, and built?

My guess is never— or you can't remember.

Intentionally recognizing what you've achieved and accomplished is your starting point in the race toward a winning life.

When you know what winning feels like, you take more actions that align with winning.

Winning feels amazing. Pride. Accomplishment. Hope. Energy. Fulfillment. Contentment.

Winning is achieving.

I want to win. Likely, you want those winning feelings too.

Winning is personal. It's an inside game, not an outside need for validation.

Winning is not an entitlement.

No one is entitled to win. No one deserves it.

Winning comes from intention.

Winning comes from devotion to discipline.

Whether we are talking about winning at work, winning in your business, or winning the day, you've got to be in it to win it. (Yes, I just used an old New York Lottery tag line. But it makes the point!)

Cliché, maybe, but you have to be in the game to win the game of life.

Are you showing up each day by design or by default?

By design wins the day every time.

How much time do you spend thinking about and designing the winning game of your life? I'm not talking about simply wishing for it to happen.

Showing up by design comes from intentional thoughts that only you can create. Your thoughts are what generate your feelings and put you into action to produce the winning results you want.

What will have you showing up by design as your best today?

Intentionally designing your day will give you focus. The strategic multiplier is that it builds momentum and motivation to achieve the BIG win of life.

Getting frustrated, impatient, or annoyed at what's not working wastes energy. Squandering energy like that simply holds you back and is demotivating. It creates momentum in the wrong direction.

Choosing your thoughts is not random. It's intentional.

Intentional creation doesn't come sometime next week or when you get a free moment. Intentional creation must have a common place in your weekly calendar. For me, intentional thought creation is a daily practice in my journal that shows up in my calendar and results.

As the 'C.E.O. of Me,' you get to choose the thoughts that serve you and what you want to create for yourself.

Living an extraordinary life comes from intentionally creating it.

What intentions will you set for today, tomorrow and the next day?

Perfectly Miserable

I achieved C-suite status after decades of hard work and an insatiable need to succeed. I thought the higher up the ladder, and with the earned experience, that work would get more manageable. It would be easier to get things done, and it wouldn't feel so hard all of the damn time. I kept telling myself that if I worked harder, things would come together.

I looked happy, put together, and in love with life, but inside I wanted something different. What was missing? Why was it all so hard? On paper, I was perfect. When in reality, I was perfectly miserable. The inner me didn't match my outer me. Spinning on the daily hamster wheel had become my default. It was an excellent excuse for not dealing with how and what I was feeling

Change comes when you are open to new thinking to find greater clarity around what you want and, ultimately, more joy for yourself.

Thinking the same way produces the same results. You've likely heard the definition of insanity as doing the same thing over and over and expecting different results.

What if you changed your thoughts in pursuit of new results?

Awareness is where it starts. Your mind can only shift when you first become aware. When I decided I'd had enough, I slowed down and did the work to uncover what kept me from where I wanted to be.

I started with my thoughts, and, oh boy, there were many of them. Most were negative, dismissive, and diminishing. Thoughts that had me comparing myself to others and thoughts that required something that I had not fully defined.

What was non-existent were thoughts that began with what if, why not, and what's possible.

To imagine what was possible, I looked in the rear-view mirror to self-reflect on my career, my achievements, what worked, and what didn't. I declared a bold vision for my future and I've risen with confidence and clarity.

Do I have it all together? Not even close. Someone once commented on my cool and calm demeanor. If she could be a fly on the wall inside my head, she would see that I'm a work in progress.

Being a work in progress means working toward my purpose each day. I stumble, fall, and take many tiny steps each week. Some steps take me forward and some back, but they are all taken intentionally and toward possibility.

There are weeks when it feels like I'm not moving fast enough. But those weeks are filled with more joy.

Get started by acknowledging all you've created. You might hate giving yourself credit as most people do. That thinking is the same thinking that will get you the same results. Instead, pay close attention to what has worked for you—the wins, both big and small—and write them down with specificity.

Make a list:

- 10 big surprises around how you've handled the roughest times.
- 10 moments of joy: this month, this year, in your life.
- 10 experiences you would do again given the chance.
- 10 things you learned this past year.
- 10 opportunities you created.
- 10 things you are grateful for today.

What is the story of your 10s? With your answers, look for the red thread of thought in them. With that story, you can begin writing your next chapter.

Are You a Dreamer or a Doer?

Dreams come from an open mind where you can see the possibilities for yourself and your future.

On his podcast, leadership guru John Maxwell shared that if you ask a room full of people to raise their hands if they had dreams when they were growing up, 100% of hands would go up.

John's next question for the room, *"How many of you are living your dream right now?"* A few hands go up.

John's final question, *"How many of you have achieved your dreams?"* Even fewer hands are raised.

What is the difference between people who achieve their dreams and those who don't?

A dreamer dreams while stagnating in the intoxication of wishful, hopeful thinking.

Doers intentionally work to get clear on their dreams and take action to make them a reality. They move their goals out of their head, commit them to paper, begin making commitments, and take steps towards achieving them. Doers have a plan.

Far too many people do not plan for their future. They continue to dream and hope those dreams will miraculously materialize. Some wait for someone to tell them what their plan should be. Some plan in their head, and only in their head, and guess what, just like their dreams, their plans don't get executed.

People spend more time planning their vacations than they do making a plan for their extraordinary life.

Think about that.

Sometimes we think we've made a plan.

"I am going to lose the weight this time. I will go to the gym. I will eat less."

We declare New Year's resolutions, yet after a few weeks of going to the gym—and a few more salads—February arrives, and the scale has not budged, or worse, it has gone in the other direction.

A lack of a concrete plan leads to a lack of tangible results.

Unmet plans have a double-whammy. You don't reach your goal, and your disappointment triggers negative self-talk—a plunge into a shame spiral and feelings of defeat.

Doers make promises to themselves that they do not break.

Doers write down their plans in detail. They make them measurable and build accountability. Doers share their dream and their plan with someone they know has their interest at heart and wants them to be happy.

Dr. Gail Matthews, a psychology professor at the Dominican University in California, recently studied the art and science of goal setting. She found that you are 42% more likely to achieve your goals and dreams, simply by writing them down on a regular basis.

Those are the kind of odds you want.

Get out of your comfort zone and away from that fear and talk of the irrational inner critic, and, instead, share your big plans.

Doers don't get distracted by the irrational
inner critic and negative self-talk.

"I don't know how," and "I might fail" are examples of the irrational inner critic talking. The mindless and irrational inner critic thinks it is protecting you from failure. Previous disappointments and self-imposed limiting beliefs feed the negative talk.

When you change your perspective, you'll change your life from one full of dreams to one full of possibility and action.

Anything is possible when you commit to yourself, commit it to paper and commit it to someone else. Your dreams get closer with planning, sharing, and executing.

Big dreams come true as a result of consistent small decisions and small steps, which compound, like interest, into big things.

Do you have a dream to one day write a book? What is stopping you from opening the computer or taking pen to paper today?

Writing 100 words daily, over 333 days (less than a year), is enough to publish a book. That's only 20 minutes a day. Stop scrolling Instagram and start using your time. Turn your dreams into your next great accomplishment. Don't have the time? Wake up

20 minutes earlier or write for 20 minutes before bed. Write on the train commute to work. You can find 20 minutes.

Plans are not just a vision board. Vision boards get you psyched up, but without a plan of action, they are merely dreams on a board. My vision statements have given me the encouragement and confidence to live my extraordinary life.

Doers — those who achieve their dreams — plan with intention.

That means:

1. Plans are outlined with small steps and small decisions.

2. Those small steps are measurable, achievable, and repeatable.

3. Those small decisions are not put off by worry due to size or expectations but are made after carefully considering the pros and cons in pursuit of continually moving forward.

4. Momentum begins outside of the comfort zone. Small steps and small decisions are small, but that does not mean they should keep you in your comfort zone. To achieve any dream requires pushing out of your comfort zone. Each time you do, you gain more experience to help you build confidence.

5. Plans need to have intention, action, and — most of all — discipline. Discipline produces new habits. Positive habits are like gifts to ourselves, an unconscious fuel, giving you time back.

Get out of your head and into the life where your dreams become your extraordinary reality.

Find that 20 minutes today. Put your dreams down on paper. Feed them with possibilities. Turn what if into what is.

This companion activity will get you started putting your extra-ordinary future in writing, download link here:

christinalangdon.com/success

More Business, Less Busy-ness

I'm so busy!

I don't like it when people say, "I'm busy."

And I like it even less when I say, "I'm busy."

But we all do it.

Nothing changes when you tell people you are busy.

Busy is a thought.

It's a thought that feels bad, punitive, and overwhelming. It compounds negativity.

And when we tell people we are busy; it doesn't make us feel any better.

So, how about intentionally reframing it?

Next time you want to say "I'm busy," instead try saying "I'm in demand," and notice how you feel.

The only way to change being busy is to change how you think about being busy.

What creates busy thoughts?

To-Do lists are traps for busy bees. But you already know that because once you've checked an item off your list another one follows. And then another. And there's always more to do, especially in leadership.

The next time you write a list, ask yourself if it includes whatever is most important to you, your business, and your future ambitions or is it simply a list of things to get done today?

Look at it through the lens of these questions:

• Does it have you working 'on' your business instead of 'in' the business?
• Does it list the stuff you like and want to prioritize?
• Does it reflect the things that are investments in who you want to become?

Thinking about how you invest in your future is a much better thought than busy thoughts.

So, why not reframe your To-Do list to a 'To-My Future' list?

As part of my morning routine, I write down three priorities crucial to pursuing my future ambitions. I use my morning time to super-think and center myself around what I want most.

Doing this each day has a compounding effect that helps suffocate busy-ness. It creates positive momentum and motivation and builds confidence.

The To-Dos will get done. If not today, then tomorrow. Today, prioritize creating your To-My Future list.

Another trap of busyness is your calendar. Allowing the day's meetings to become the centerpiece of your organizational system prevents you from becoming who you want to become unless you plan your calendar from your To-My Future list.

When the calendar controls you, you put off writing your To-My Future list.

Begin your weekly calendaring with your To-My Future list as a baseline. When your calendar starts with your future priorities, you will manage meetings and To-Dos around them.

I worked with someone who blocked out two hours of his day every day. On our shared online calendar, he titled those hours, 'Me Time.' I naively made fun of him for doing it. He is now a successful Chief Revenue Officer. He dedicated time in pursuit of his highest priorities. He got sh*t done. And as a result? He's now the sh*t!

Years ago, on any given day, I would have 20, 30, and 40 tabs open on both my Chrome and Safari browsers. It was one symptom of being busy in my mind. I committed to closing the tabs—most of them—and creating a calendar filled with my future aspirations to banish busyness for good.

BECOMING

I Am

I am my word.

I am like no one else.

I am boldly creating even when uncertain.

I am in pursuit of an extraordinary life.

I had an exceptional second quarter in 2022, and was curious about what made this quarter different. I evaluated the quarter and couldn't put my finger on anything in particular or extraordinary that I'd done versus previous quarters.

While I rarely go back and read the pages in my journal, I was curious about what I was thinking and writing at the time to help give me insight.

What I saw in my morning journal pages was a lot of work on organizing my thoughts. Also on those pages were daily entries of 'I am' statements. Several months back I had read about the 'I am' practice in the book *The Ultimate Coach* by Amy Hardison and Alan D. Thompson and began incorporating it into my morning routine.

Who you are being is everything.

My 'I am' statements are an expression of that. Writing them has me taking ownership of who I am and how I see my future. They are reflections and reminders of my identity and the accompanying behaviors.

I consistently showed up for my morning writing time with these statements.

The Ultimate Coach begins with Coach Steve Hardison asking the reader to answer a list of writing prompts before you read the book. I did, and I hope you will, too, as I believe now with 100% certainty that writing my "I am" statements were the source, the difference, and the energy in elevating my performance.

I retrained my brain with my conviction of who I wanted to be.

The funny thing about the brain, and backed by neuroscience research, is that when you imagine a possibility, the brain cannot tell the difference between what you've imagined and if it's happened.

My 'I am' statements helped me build belief in myself and my work elevating how I showed up personally and professionally.

The art and science of journaling is a proven performance enhancer when done consistently and with intention. Just ask Oprah, Arianna Huffington, Bill Gates, and Tim Ferris, who journal.

———

"I don't journal to be productive. I don't do it to find great ideas or put down prose I can later publish. These pages aren't intended for anyone but me. It's the most cost-effective therapy I've ever found."

-Tim Ferris, Entrepreneur, and Author

———

You may be reading this thinking: *I can't. Not me. I don't have time.* If notable high performers and billionaires are believers, why not you? This was the question I asked myself when I resisted journaling.

You can retrain your brain in 10 minutes a day.

When I journal, I see what I didn't before.

When I journal, I see with more clarity.

When I journal, new thoughts surface that I likely would not have discovered had I not put pen to paper.

These new thoughts have changed my business.

Journaling helps me navigate energetic conversations ahead of time.

As I write my three pages daily, new concepts, inspiration, and points of view emerge. Thoughts magically find their way onto the page.

I always have a separate sheet of paper next to me. Ideas come up along with some 'To-Dos' that I may have forgotten in the rush of the day.

You may be thinking that all you'll write will be negative. That it will be too much complaining. Think about it: better there, where you can leave it on the page, rather than carrying it into your day.

Writing daily helps you unload the baggage of the day, make sense of it, and focus on what you want to create.

You will find the days you skip journaling will be the days you need it most.

Journaling shifts a cluttered mind to a managed mind. That's retraining the brain to serve you.

I start by writing my 'I am' statements. Then, I write about my previous day, what worked, what didn't, and what I would do differently. I also write about who I'm becoming. I close with writing about my coming day and what outcomes I will have when I show up on my 'A' game.

For me, the pen to paper frees my mind to unload and create. I don't feel the same impact when I'm typing.

That's my practice.

What do you want your journal practice to look like?

Oh, the stories you will write, the places you will go, the life you will create. The blank pages provide space for a managed mind, clarity, and a place to design what you want.

Ten minutes a day may change your life.

If you want additional inspiration, this resource gives you daily inspirational thoughts to write about:

christinalangdon.com/success

You're Invited to Create the Impossible

"You can't connect the dots looking forward;
you can only connect them looking backward.
So you have to trust that the dots will somehow
connect in your future. You have to trust in
something—your gut, destiny, life, karma,
whatever. This approach has never let me down,
and it has made all the difference in my life."

-Steve Jobs, Apple Founder, 2005 Stanford
University Commencement Speech

If you have not written your responses to the '10s' exercise from the chapter titled Perfectly Miserable, do that as a first step in creating the impossible for yourself. Your answers to those questions are the seeds of your impossible goals waiting to be mined, recognized, and celebrated.

With your '10s,' let's explore and go deeper with thought-provoking questions around three simple concepts. For each of your '10s', ask yourself:

What if?

Why not?

Why is that important?

Declaring your bold vision takes time, thought, exercise, and commitment. Break through the impossible with this exercise in possibilities. Commit to not breaking promises to ourselves this time. Choose to be audacious and deliberate.

Start today by committing it to paper. When you do, your potential for success will exponentially increase.

Take this work deeper with The Possibility Formula exercise that can be downloaded from this link:

christinalangdon.com/success

You Are Made for More

Are you at a point in your life where you've achieved success but are asking, Is this it?"

I was raised with all sorts of life expectations from graduating high school, attending college, and landing that first job out of school in pursuit of a successful career. There were also expectations for finding my one love to walking down the aisle to living a joyful married life. Expected next was having kids, all while perfectly juggling the job. If you are like me, somewhere between working full-time and raising children, I asked myself, "Is this it?"

As I shared in the opening of this book, I was fortunate in my career to become a media publisher and get as far as the C-suite, but something kept gnawing at me. I still wanted more.

More what? I wasn't sure what more looked like or how I'd define it. I wanted to make a difference and leave a mark, but how, and what exactly?

For years, my circumstances—single mom, young kids, expectations from others—were my excuses not to explore, not to consider, not to even think about wanting more.

I kept waiting for something to happen to me.

Out of frustration, impatience, and a disappointment in myself, I decided that if I wanted something to change, I was in charge of deciding.

Have you fallen into the trap of not wanting for yourself?

Raising kids while juggling a job and other responsibilities has an effect that can lead to you putting yourself last on the list, especially with the expectations our culture puts on women, moms, and female business leaders.

Are you thinking:

• Now is not the right time.
• My bank balance needs to be higher.
• When the kids graduate.

"The ability to *create the future*
instead of responding to circumstances
is an undervalued superpower."

-Rich Litvin, Coach and Author

Read that powerful quote again. It says so much in very few words. Your life is not created by circumstances but how you respond to them is what will create your future.

I want to share with you what I wish I had discovered earlier.

DO NOT waste your pretty years.

I'm not sure where that statement originated from but it came up a lot in conversations with my single girlfriends when I was dating, especially after one of us had a bad date.

Your pretty years are the years when your wisdom and talent are at their peak, and your voice has something important to say.

If you are itching for more, why not start by exploring what more looks like for you?

What if your wildest dreams were not dreams but big plans simply waiting for you to get started?

Don't waste your pretty years.

Get to it. You deserve it.

Give Yourself an "A" Ahead of Time

What if you could give yourself an A grade just for being you?

What if you could wake up each day and, before the day begins, and decide to give yourself an A for the day to come? Give yourself permission to decide on a positive outcome before succumbing to the daily grind and intentionally choose a thought that would have you making a difference without question, comparison, doubt, or second thoughts.

When failure is impossible, you can be free to be your best, without question or second-guessing, to create what's amazingly possible for you.

The intentionally granted A grade lifts you off the success or failure ladder, away from a world of measurements, and into one of possibilities, as written in the book *The Artist's Way* by Julia Cameron.

This outcome-based thinking allows you to reach for your highest potential.

It's not about productivity but a mindset that will make you more productive.

Imagine how different your world would be if you woke up feeling confident that today you would be at your best for yourself and those around you.

When you go all in with an A grade you eliminate the clutter that holds you in doubt, keeps you locked in judgment, and prevents you from being decisive.

When you give yourself an A you let your expertise, experience, and intuition guide you.

An A is the best kind of love you can gift yourself. Loving yourself first is the most loving thing you can do for others.

Then ask, "Who needs me on my A game today?"

Being in service to others is another gift you can give yourself.

Give yourself that A today. It will show up for you in so many ways.

———

"It's about having the cojones to show up as
the brightest, happiest, badassiest version of
yourself, whatever that looks like to you."

-Jen Sincero, Author, *You Are a Badass: How to Stop
Doubting Your Greatness and Start Living an Awesome Life*

———

My badass self assigned me an A grade just before I wrote this.

A Look Back to Move Forward

How you see the world becomes your world.

_____

"If you don't control it, why worry about it?
Because you don't control it.
And if you do control it, why worry about it?
Because you control it."

–Warren Rustand, C.E.O., Public Speaker, and Author

_____

What can you control?

Sometimes, looking back at the path taken helps objectively observe the good you've brought to this world. This is actually a fuel source to create more of the results you want. It is in your control and is a proven performance booster.

Acknowledge your accomplishments, achievements, and impact. Don't think this is a waste of time or take a cursory review. Think of this time as time invested in you and your future; time well spent auditing the life you've already created and is uniquely you.

A forward-thinking leader uses their past as evidence to become a more decisive leader.

Your resume and LinkedIn profile are public and flat reflections of your career and how you want to be seen by others.

What about rethinking your career history that comes from a place of profound celebration? If not you, then who?

This is not shameless self-promotion but an exercise in building belief in yourself and showcasing what you've created and accomplished. Call it a mining exercise to forage for hidden superpowers. It's a proven performance booster to help you let go of diminishing thoughts and see—really see—what you've achieved.

The takeaway will likely have you feeling more confident and even joyful about your impact. It will also help you inform your path forward. With awareness comes clarity, and with clarity comes more control over how you show up.

By thoughtfully taking the time to map out your story in full detail, you will begin to see clues, patterns, and a compass that will guide you forward.

Take out a sheet of paper, lay it vertically, and draw a horizontal line across the middle of the page. On the line, write the name of each job you have held as far back as your first job. (You may need more than one sheet.) Above each job, in column format going up to the top of the page, list all the job responsibilities as you might find them in a job description.

Below the horizontal line in a column under each job name, list how it felt when you were feeling your best, enjoying the work, and being in a flow state. Also list the little things you remember most about who you were at the time, what you were most proud of, and what you learned. Describe the environment and the culture. How you honed your skills and leveled up your expertise. What worked and what didn't. I also recommend listing your 'never agains.' Give each job a grade between 1-10, with ten being the best.

Each job, job title, business, and product launch has been transformational in some way for you. They have shaped your story by influencing your growth, development, expertise, knowledge, and learning. And they are all unique to you.

After you've mapped it out, step away for a bit. Take a break and come back to it with fresh eyes.

Go through a diagnostic with these questions:
• What stands out?
• What surprises you?
• What fits you?
• What doesn't fit?
• Where did you put your best foot forward?
• Which roles were most instrumental in getting to where you are today?
• Which roles were most influential on the leader you are today?

Go back to each question's answer and ask why?

As you look back on your success, what do you see? What areas of focus, activities, and experiences do you want to leverage and bring with you in the future?

This exercise will move you away from the words on your resume and into a more profound recognition of what is important to you.

In doing this exercise, I rediscovered that I was an early leader and that there was consistency in my drive to teach and inspire others to be better.

Even as far back as a seventeen-year-old in the eleventh grade —working as head waitress at a local Italian restaurant and as the nighttime supervisor for a research company—I felt immense satisfaction from showing others how to make more money. Educating my colleagues on how to earn higher tips at the restaurant and generate more commissions on completed research surveys was both satisfying and rewarding. I also saw that, in times of crisis, I was able to manage situations and help others to manage them better. These examples provide incredible insight to see what would become one of my superpowers.

Doing a deep diagnostic of how I experienced each job and showed up helped me know myself better.

Give it a try. Don't wait for the rewrite of the resume. After doing this exercise, you may be inspired to take your resume in a new direction.

How you see the world today becomes your world tomorrow.

Seeing an audit of all you've accomplished may just be the thing that brings clarity to the direction of your extraordinary life.

Your Dream C.E.O. Role

To grow your business, you must develop the person running it.

To lead, you must first become the person who leads themselves first.

To experience less struggle and find more joy in the process of doing it all, you must believe you can.

When was the last time you wrote your job description?

You may be thinking, why would I waste my precious time writing a list of what I do every day?

Well...

- You need to know what you are doing.
- You need to know why you are doing it.
- You need to know what you don't want to do anymore.
- Your team needs to know what they can expect from you.
- Your clients want to know how to work with you.

Most of all, knowing brings accountability to who you are becoming and what you want for your business.

When uncertainty and overwhelm take over, it may be driven by a lack of clarity, brought about by the daily grind. Lack of clarity perpetuates a state of being which keeps us locked in the same behaviors and experiencing the same results.

When work isn't getting done, team members are not aligned, and results are not happening, go back to the basics.

I'm not suggesting you write a job description for hiring purposes.

I'm suggesting you do it to determine who you are and who you want to become.

Be sure to:

• Scope your complete list of your responsibilities.
• State what and who you are accountable for/to.
• Define or outline your measurements for success.
• Write with specificity.
• Describe how you execute tasks.
• Record the results you are creating.

Auditing your role like this may sound tedious, but it is revealing.

One client of mine took the task of writing his/her job description and job descriptions for each member of his/her seventeen-person team. They then interviewed each other in a workshop setting and asked:

• What do you like most about your role?
• What do you wish more people knew about your role?
• What do you want to do more of?

The result was a huge morale boost. The team no longer stepped on each other's toes, and accountability skyrocketed. My client, with that increased clarity about her role as the leader, doubled her revenue and readily took on Series A funding.

The next step in this exercise may be the most important. Review today's job description and now write your future job description.

This exercise will lay the foundation for your Dream C.E.O. position.

Put your eye on the prize and create it.

• What will you be doing?
• Who will you be doing it with?
• What results will you be responsible for creating?
• What can your team count on you for?
• What can your clients count on you for?
• Who will you be?

When you started your current role, you dreamt of success, fun, joy, earning expectations, and a desire to achieve and feel accomplished; translating that into a plan for your future begins with writing it down.

I dream of delivering massive value and having an enormous impact. I've written my C.E.O.-of-Me job description and had so much fun writing my Dream C.E.O. role.

Now that I've written it, I've started becoming it.

I've also changed how I spend my time pursuing it.

After putting my job description on paper, I can measure every decision based on who I want to become and what I want for my business. Writing it down has given me a very clear action plan.

Inspiration is the Holy Grail of Enthusiasm

"Inspiration is a three-beers-in guitar solo.
It yields a moment of galvanizing energy
and vision that precedes motivation and
shoves it into action. With motivation, we
take hold of an idea and run with it. With
inspiration, an idea takes hold of us."

–Scott Mautz, Author, *Find the Fire,*
Make It Matter, and Leading from the Middle

For me, being inspired is the fuel that feeds my soul and my very being. We all want to be inspired.

Do you know what inspires you?

Understanding what inspires you will help you live a more inspired and extraordinary life.

The byproduct of inspiration will likely inspire others. That's a wonderful thing.

Declaring a bold vision for your life and moving into action begins with the thoughts that inspire us to be bold. Take action, change our perspective, and go all in.

So, what inspires you? When you know, you'll know the powerful feelings that will move you from thinking about what's possible to taking massive action.

Here are a few things that inspire me.

A woman I know wants to be known for her accomplishments, not her disabilities. She has a rare disease that has left her with 5% of her eyesight and severe hearing loss. She navigates daily hurdles to deliver massive value and impact in her work. A good reminder that when I think something is hard, it could be harder for someone else.

In my twenties, Martha Stewart told me to learn something new every day and then teach it to someone else. That advice has become a personal mantra for me. I'm inspired to learn almost anything (technology excluded!), and I'm driven to share what I've learned with anyone who will listen.

I'm inspired by women who stand up boldly and unabashedly share their powerful voices—make their opinions known, ask interesting questions, and offer probing thoughts. I admire women who are not afraid to stand up and have others hear them roar. I want to model that behavior. That's living proof of the impact of inspiration.

I'm inspired by visionary and purpose-driven leaders, founders, and bold thinkers who dream of changing the world and then pursue those dreams to make it happen. They don't waste their time comparing themselves with others and they are steadfast in their pursuit of breaking through to the impossible. What's your impossible?

I'm inspired by the unconditional love I receive from those in my life who want nothing more than to see me succeed.

I'm inspired by the optimists who always see the glass half full. Speed bumps are merely moments for them to double down and carry on. They leave feelings of entitlement to others while creating their own success.

I'm inspired by those who organize and plan their life based on their desired results. My coach shared with me her detailed calendar. It's mapped out months ahead where she plans to spend her time writing her books, working with clients, and taking vacations. Where do you want to spend your time? I'm inspired by what I saw to create my future ahead of time.

I'm inspired by all of those leaders who moved through COVID with grace and grit. I'm inspired by those who saw the pandemic as an experience to rediscover and double down on what they wanted.

I'm inspired by my kids every day. Years ago, as I waited for my son to get discharged from ACL surgery, I was reminded of how much his resilience inspires me. Teddy has overcome a lot including a broken back and three prior surgeries. I'm inspired by many who have overcome and continue to manage their lives despite health challenges.

These are just a few of my inspirations. I'm so grateful for the role models in my life who light me up and continue to give me the energy to become who I'm becoming.

Take a look at who and what inspires you.

Your answers will move you to more of what you want for yourself.

Why Do Some People Achieve So Much and Others Don't?

Have you ever wondered why some people achieve so much with their lives and others don't?

As you plan for the year ahead, put YOU at the center. As your goals and possibilities evolve, so will you.

As soon as you evolve, you start becoming your future self.

Ask yourself, who do I want to become? It has become the most important question in my life and might be just as powerful for you. More often than not, when I ask people who they want to become, they are surprised, resistant, or say, I don't know. They are unsure or worried that replying wouldn't be humble. Many simply do not know who they would become if they could become it.

Here's my list of who I want to become.

Someone who:
• Wants to create massive impact and massive value.
• Manages her calendar in pursuit of control and intention.
• Prioritizes space to grow and engage in self-care.
• Knows that life is hard and knows that's to be expected.
• Doesn't rush to judgments and is more patient.
• Comes from a place of curiosity.
• Desires mastery while knowing she's a work in progress.
• Works to manage stress while giving herself compassion and grace.
• Is enough, even on her worst days.
• Shows up consistently and authentically.

With this list, I can now look for opportunities to work on creating my most extraordinary life.

My most extraordinary life, along with my audacious and outrageous goals, is my trifecta.

With a focus on and recognition of who I want to become, I can begin becoming.

Who do you want to become?

Start solving, understanding, and answering that for yourself.

"The next version of you is the one who will pursue the ambition all the previous versions were unable to accomplish."

-Bob Goff, Author, *Dream Big: Know What You Want, Why You Want It, and What You're Going to Do About It*

Creators & Procrasta-Learners

If you had the choice of being a reporter, a consumer, or a creator, which would you choose?

Let me give you more context to the question.

The Reporter

When I worked at Fast Company, the sales leader who worked with me knew the business well, was respected by clients, and his team enjoyed working with him.

When I asked for his thoughts on a new product launch, I got what I would call a non-answer. He shared where we were, what they tried before, and what was currently on the market. He gave me a status report with little opinion, insight, or discovery.

In our weekly sales meetings, he would share business updates, week-over-week changes, and current business standings. Like a weatherman standing in front of the green screen, he shared a general forecast with highlights and lowlights and referenced potential storms and their severity.

He was a reporter.

The Consumer

People share they are stuck or have trouble building momentum.

An audit of their time reveals they are consuming in pursuit of inspiration, guidance, growth or the next big thing. They are working hard, reading leadership and self-help books, listening to webinars and podcasts, and taking classes. They are spending time in pursuit of a light bulb moment or simply to learn the thing that will help get them out of feeling stuck and in a rut.

They are procrasta-learners.

I heard the word procrasta-learner on a podcast that I wish I could remember. The procrasta-learner is a consumer whose consumption is misplaced productivity. Consumption as an avoidance tactic. Procrasta-learners think that the more they learn, listen, or read will get them ready to take action and do something with it all.

Consuming is easier to do than what you are avoiding. Consuming feels safer than the work to take action to get unstuck.

To a degree, we are all consumers. Knowing when we are over-consuming and when it's time to move to put what we've consumed into action is a key to moving us forward.

Are you consuming or are you waiting? Waiting can be a delay tactic brought on by fear. Fear often presents itself right before moments of personal growth.

If you think you fall into procrasta-learner tendencies, ask yourself: why am I waiting for an outside source to help me make an inside decision?

Learning can be motivating, but unless you grow from it and put learning into action, you simply stay in place or fall further into a rut.

The Creators

Creators tap into what they know, whom they know, and who they are to create what they want for themselves, their business, and their career.

Creators are deliberate, calculating how they prioritize their time and effort toward their desired outcome.

Dr. Somi Javaid, ObGyn MD, grew frustrated, wanting more for patients, particularly those struggling with menopause and sexual dysfunction. She saw a gender gap in healthcare and a lack of access to exceptional healthcare. She believes women need a safe place where they feel empowered and educated about their choices. It didn't exist, so she created it. Dr. Javaid opened her first office in 2015, and as of this writing, HerMD now offers in-person and telehealth healthcare in 6 states, with more planned in the coming years. The demand is great. In 2021, patients traveled from 33 states and 3 countries to be treated at HerMD. Each step of the way, she created. New standards. Custom protocols. A new definition for exceptional healthcare.

Whether leading a team of hundreds or a business of one, creators invest their time in becoming the leader they want to role model, developing their business, and putting action to what they have consumed.

When creators report on their business, they do it with creation in mind. They share that because of a decline in revenue (reporting) and with that new platform they've researched (consuming), they are implementing a new marketing initiative (creating). This process is called consuming to create.

Creators learn, act, audit, and evaluate for generative outcomes.

Where we spend our time is what we prioritize. Look back at last week's calendar for when you reported, consumed, and took action to create.

Would you rather create and fail than consume and stay safe?

A Life Full of Green Lights

"You write your own life script." This was one of my mom's replies if I was complaining about someone, something, or a circumstance.

When I finally was ready to listen, when I was ready to hear it, the world opened up to me. I do write my own life script.

In his book, *Greenlights*, Matthew McConaughey writes that his life story is "about how to catch more yeses in a world of nos and how to recognize when a no might actually be a yes,"

He continues, "This is a book about catching greenlights and realizing that the yellows and reds eventually turn green."

–Matthew McConaughey,
Actor and Author, *Greenlights*

Green lights. We all want more of them.

What would change for you if you believed 100% that the yellow and red lights in your life would turn green? Read that back again.

To catch more green lights in your life, start by identifying the green lights you've already created. What makes them green for you?

What if those green lights—if you doubled down on them—could become a flywheel to more green lights? Focusing on what's already working will make a significant impact.

Now, identify where your red lights are and ask yourself, what would need to happen to change course to hit fewer of them?

What if your red lights were just one decision away from turning green?

What if your red lights were simply the result of old beliefs that are no longer true or relevant today? Think about creating your future from today, not from the past.

Now to the yellow lights. Consider that what you see as a caution signal might be fear in disguise. Acting cautiously out of a fear of failure is a dream killer. Failure is a teacher. Don't let it stop you.

Fear of the unknown often prevents you from writing your life script to include more green lights. Fear is often a mask for what we desire most. How quickly do you default to no? That quick response to an unknown might be your next green light.

Frequently, yellow lights surround what we procrastinate on or avoid, and it is those things that—if prioritized—could bring about successive green lights.

Martha Stewart received a red light when Time Inc. which, at the time, owned the Martha Stewart brand. Time Inc. said no to expanding the magazine brand into products and television. But that red light didn't stop her—quite the opposite. It drove her to create a new future for herself and her namesake brand. She formed a multi-year, pre-paid merchandising partnership with Kmart, the big box store, to fund the purchase of her brand back from Time Inc.

Red lights only stop you for as long as you allow them to.

Steve Job's yellow light came when he dropped out of Reed College after one semester as he felt his time was better spent elsewhere. His green light came when he sat in on a calligraphy class the semester after he dropped out. Calligraphy inspired the landmark digital typefaces of the Macintosh computer that is now found on most all branded computers.

Curiosity and creativity are energy sources that will turn red lights green.

A personal example is my cancer diagnosis on April Fools' Day 2019. It was a red light that stopped me dead in my tracks. The forced slow down and quiet time during treatment gave me time to decide what I wanted most for my life. It was time to write a new script for my life. While not an easy road, I've now seen more green lights than yellow or red.

Green lights are not automatic.

No one is entitled to green lights.

Green light making is a practice that requires consistency, discipline, and reflection.

Green lights come to those who do the work. To those who put in the time and effort.

Think about how you can change your trajectory when you believe that today's yellow and red lights were just waiting for you to turn them green.

RESILIENCE

Detours & U-Turns

I schedule think time for my business at the start of every week. During that time without fail, I'll receive a FaceTime call from my son, Jack, or an urgent email from a client, and there's always that call from the pantry to grab that bag of truffle popcorn. Interruptions are the one thing I can count on.

Daily interruptions distract you, zap your focus, and create havoc in your well-planned day. You may feel sabotaged, discouraged, and/or regretful from all of the distractions. Then you judge yourself for not being in control of both the thoughts and the distractions.

Distractions are costly. Distractions delay or prevent you from reaching your highest potential. You blame distractions for your lack of focus or for your being stuck.

Consider that distractions are simply the detours of your day.

U-turns can put you back on track.

Instead of a detour taking you off course, why not consider a distraction as a green light to take a U-turn?

Answering emails as soon as they hit the inbox—as if each one is an emergency—is a huge distraction. And if you don't answer them immediately, perhaps you start thinking about how busy you are because of all the emails, which only adds to the distraction. Busy is a negative thought to recognize. Turning the idea of "I'm so busy" into a more powerful one, like "I'm in demand," will course-correct you back to what's essential. That's one type of a

U-turn. The empowered thought feels so much better than the negative thought of being so busy.

With conscious thought and being open to what's possible, you decide whether to detour or take a U-turn. I read about this concept in The Artist's Way, and I'm putting a twist on it.

The speed of your U-turn determines how fast you reset, renew, and get back to what's important. Here are three steps to keep you on track.

Awareness

Taking back your power from distraction starts by becoming aware.

• Make a list of what distracts you; all of the things that get in your way.
• Look for the triggers. The messy, disorganized mind full of thoughts is a distraction caused by stress, overwork, and indecision.
• Search for the bad habits and patterns that make distraction 'easy.'

Park it

What are your three priorities for the day? With that as your guide, most distractions can be parked. Rank your list of detours. Park anything that isn't relevant to your three priorities. Consider calendaring your park it list; with your priorities as your guide, almost every distraction can then be parked. Reserving time on the calendar to get to your distractions will allow you to quickly U-turn back to what's essential.

Get Help

When you are most distracted, ask for help, even if you hate asking for help. Get the needed support. It may give you a new perspective and the space to make a U-turn and get back on course. Let go of thoughts like, "I need to do this myself" or "Only I can do this." Your ego never rewards you.

Is this easy? No.

Is it worth it? Yes.

Creative U-Turns

You have the choice to take the detour or take a U-turn. A U-turn is committing to yourself and all the possibilities that await you in your most extraordinary life. It's an active choice to not fall into distraction mode. I'm not saying it's possible to eliminate every distraction, but if you can increase your awareness as to how you are spending your time, you can choose to park it and take that U-turn.

My Distraction Audit

When I audited my daily distractions, I discovered that 2pm was my most distracted time of the day. To fix this, I set a 'Bring More Joy' reminder notification on my cell phone that pops up on my screen each day at 2pm. This visualization prompt is a reminder of what's important. This reminds me to reset, refocus, and renew my commitment to myself and my priorities. It gives me that kick I need most days.

Confidence Building Blocks

You are looking for confidence in all of the wrong places.

When I was in the emergency room at Memorial Sloane Kettering (MSK), 24 hours after I was diagnosed with AML Leukemia, a stream of doctors asked me the same series of questions about my symptoms.

My family and two close friends surrounded me. What I saw in their eyes mirrored my own feelings. Terrified by the diagnosis. An utter loss of control at the thought of undergoing excruciating treatment to save my life for the next year. Not surviving was also playing on repeat in my head.

Then Dr. Jai Park walked in. He was calm and had an ease about him. He asked me the same series of questions and then gave me a life-saving thought. Dr. Park very matter-of-factly shared:

You don't come to MSK to be treated.

You come to MSK to be cured.

My thoughts quickly took a turn. I thought, Game On!

I needed to hear it and wanted to hear it, but I also wanted more.

At that moment, did I want my oncologist to be confident or competent?

What is confidence?

Confidence is a feeling.

Confidence is not a fact.

Confidence is not a result.

Confidence is not evidence of competency. Merriam-Webster's Dictionary describes competency as the ability to do something successfully or efficiently.

Confidence is not evidence of someone's competency. You can be confident and not have the competency to back it up. Think about finishing a marathon. You can be confident you will finish the marathon, but you do not have the competency of being a marathon runner until you accomplish the 26.2-mile run. Confidence and competence are two very different things.

Dr. Park has many letters after his name, and his bio includes a long list of his achievements. All facts. All results of his hard work and deepening competency.

At that moment in MSK's ER, I wanted Dr. Park to be competent to the degree he could be confident in my being cured.

Confidence is driven by competency.

If you are like most people, you've experienced these thoughts:

I've lost my confidence.

I wish I were more confident.

If I were confident, things would be different.

If I were more confident, I'd be more successful.

Waiting for confidence to get you something, or somewhere, is a trap.

You think confidence is a solution.

But the foundation of your confidence sits within your competency.

Confidence is something you want.

But what people want from you is your competence.

We all struggle with confidence at some point.

Confidence power outages come in all shapes and sizes and at all the wrong times, especially when you doing something new, often before moments of personal growth.

When your confidence is lacking, or you wish you had more of it, lean on your competency.

Leverage what you've successfully done before and build from there.

When you become more experienced, you build more competency.

Don't forget to give yourself permission to celebrate your competency as it is today. You've worked hard for it.

Make a list of your strengths including your super strengths and secret strengths.

Make a list of what you are most proud of.

Make of list of how you felt after that last thing you were proud of.

Collect (and read) a list of testimonials, reviews, and glowing emails that you've received. Then answer this question: How did I make that happen?

Now, create a Hype Folder to keep all of your answers and refer to it whenever you are hit with a confidence power outage.

When you understand that confidence is born from competence, you have all you need to build your confidence and show up more confidently.

Finding Your Voice

If you could choose one personal goal for yourself, what would that be?

This was the question I asked in a survey of entrepreneurs during a webinar, and more than 50% replied: *Find My Voice.*

Your voice is an expression of your values and beliefs that is shared with perspective and agency. Sharing authentically represents who you are and what you want.

Finding or strengthening your voice starts with listening to it

Listen to inner voice and what it's telling you about your resistance; the reasons, excuses and judgments.

Get the pen moving to start exploring and seeking your voice. Begin writing three single-lined pages every day. Over time, listen for the voice that seeps into your writing. Look for reoccurring desires, wishes, and wants.

Like the concept of journaling or not, some of the most successful leaders journal every day. If you're not doing it already, why not give it a try?

The writing prompts below will help you explore.

• Why is it important for my voice to be heard?
• What will be different with a stronger voice?
• When did I last have a positive experience using my voice?
• What will be different when I speak up?

• What impact will I make by sharing my voice?
• When will I know when I've found my voice?

Think about what other questions would help you go deeper.

I found my voice the first time I hit publish on my first Sunday Sunshine newsletter. I struggled with calling myself an expert. The irrational inner critic ran rampant, and the fear around the idea, writing, and acquiring subscribers felt much more potent than the positive possibilities.

I first needed to let go of expected judgment from others. The opinion that mattered most was mine.

I ultimately embraced the idea of a post missing the mark. Whose measuring stick would I be using? Who would decide good or bad or missing the mark?

I wanted to learn how to write consistently and with purpose. A weekly newsletter would build momentum, growth, and my business brand.

Most of all, I felt that my voice was needed. I built belief in my voice as a guide to help inspire those who chose to hear it.

The process of finding my voice was also an exercise in building my self-concept which took time. I had to be deliberate in my thinking and journaling to get comfortable and more familiar with sharing my voice. Building belief in myself, my writing, my business, and in my C.E.O. self-concept is a continual work in progress but powerfully rewarding.

One of my clients said, "I realized that I have been selling myself short, and at this point in my career, it is a huge disservice to me. Breakthrough moment! Now, I just have to find my voice."

Sharing your voice may rock a few boats or spark difficult conversations but it will allow you to emerge as the next best version of yourself.

Not sharing your voice leaves you languishing in the discomfort of personal judgment and festering in disappointment. There's the messy mind that zaps your energy and holds you in conflict with yourself.

Remember, the most influential person in your life is you, and when you recognize that influence, it's a game changer.

Using Your Voice

You were given the gift of your voice. It's unique to you. It has opinion and conviction that when quieted not only punishes you but punishes those who may learn something or need the support of hearing your voice.

When I reflect on the times in my life and career when I dragged my feet, fell short, got left behind, and disappointed myself and others, there was one common denominator: I wasn't using my voice.

If you want to strengthen your voice and the impact you want to make with it, be intentional. When you plan for your week ahead, decide ahead of time where your voice is important and where you want to show up with your voice on your 'A' game.

Look for where it might be uncomfortable to speak up, but where it's important for your voice to have a seat at the table. Decide ahead of time how to turn uncomfortable into what is possible. This gives you time to think about the impact you want to make and how you will make it. Preparation is everything and being intentional with how you will show up will support you in creating more of the outcomes you want by using your voice.

Being unintentional reinforces why you don't use your voice in the first place.

Nothing is more disquieting than discovering where your voice was needed after the fact. Don't live in regret looking back on what you wished you had said. Decide on what you will do differently next time.

Instead of thinking that you don't know what to say or that you might say something wrong, consider using your voice to engage and foster deeper connection:

- Ask questions
- Show compassion
- Give compliments
- Seek understanding
- Share your point of view
- Bring a new perspective or a new thought
- Speak with someone who needs you
- Bring your expertise
- Leave a mark
- Tell a story

Use your voice to tell your story. No one else can tell it better.

You always have a choice when you feel like your voice isn't heard or appreciated. Be intentional. Prepare. Make decisions in advance. You are uniquely you, and your voice is essential.

And, if not being heard or recognized persists, you may be in the wrong room, in the wrong job, or surrounded by the wrong people.

Direct is Beautiful

When I was leading the sales team at Martha Stewart Living Omnimedia, one of my bosses told me I was too direct.

She shared that my directness was holding me back from achieving career success. I put people off. I was harsh.

I can't remember what she said or how much I'm embellishing because whatever she verbalized left a deep and lasting mark.

Soon after, I shrunk myself to help others see me differently or 'better' than direct. I carried the perceived penalty of directness and became cautious and scripted. The new character I was playing had me feeling unsure and insecure, and, as a result, I was less effective.

To those who are labeled:

Assertive. *Keep being assertive. It's a sign of confidence.*

Bossy. *Keep leading. The world needs change agents more than ever.*

Difficult. *Stand your ground in your truth.*

Too Much. *Find the tribe that celebrates you.*

Awkward. *Believe in your uniqueness. No one is quite like you.*

Direct. *Stay authentic and transparent. People will always know where they stand with you.*

When you're feeling dismissed, raise your voice.

Most importantly, be yourself.

You are beautiful just the way you are.

I will no longer be minimized by the words of someone who could have instead shared with me the benefits of my directness. What a learning moment it could have been to help me see how I could leverage my directness to lead with even more brilliance.

My directness is a point of difference now. It's now my signature.

I'm careful to use my directness positively, not punitively. When I'm direct, people know I care deeply.

Here's to all of us bossy, demanding, loud, direct badasses.

Unstoppable in the Face of Fear

What lies on the other side of fear?

Before you push out of your comfort zone right before you walk onto that bigger stage for you or your business, you likely experience the roller coaster of fearful thoughts. You go from the depths of despair to elation.

I can't do this.

I have no clue.

What if it all goes to sh*t?

This feels yucky.

I hate not being certain.

What will others think?

What will I think?

This feels amazing.

This isn't so bad.

I did it.

That was epic!!!

This is how I felt walking across the stage to accept an award at my coaching mastermind. I did not allow the thoughts of fear to hold me back from moving through to epic.

You experience an emotion for ninety seconds which produce thoughts. Thoughts about what that emotion means.

For example, you are feeling fear, anxiety, and nervousness. Ninety seconds later, you move to thoughts of what those emotions say about you.

In doing that, you are changing whatever that emotion is into a judgment.

"I am not good enough; I suck; I'm not cut out for this."

Now, let's think about thoughts that come from the emotion of courage.

"That was amazing; I did it, that felt awesome; I'm proud of myself."

We should not be afraid to feel emotions, good or bad. They are all part of life.

But becoming aware of how you translate emotions into thoughts is powerful—possibly the gateway to a more joyful and extraordinary life.

After twelve months of treatment for AML Leukemia and after the lockdowns caused by COVID, I attended a conference that took me out of my comfort zone that required me to muster personal courage and squash that feeling of being a fraud. I felt the full spectrum of imposter emotions. With those emotions came negative thoughts I created in response to what they meant about me.

I intentionally focused on feeling courageous instead of feeling the emotions contributing to the drama and lies my irrational inner critic was yelling at me. It was a transformational week that I wouldn't have experienced had I let the fear mean something about me. I worked to understand those negative emotions did not mean anything about me as a person or my business. I chose to recognize the thoughts of fear for what they were and how they were irrationally protecting me.

Attitude is Everything

Attitude is everything. I know this firsthand after being diagnosed and treated for AML Leukemia. Throughout that process, I worked to focus on what I could control—my attitude and mindset. That's a strength of mine.

Strength doesn't have one definition.

You get to define it for yourself.

Think about the power in that, authority over yourself. You get to choose what you believe about yourself and your abilities; and leverage your strengths to show up as your best self.

In 2021, Fitbit, the wearable fitness tracker company, created an advertising campaign called, What's Strong with You? This simple turn of phrase from what's wrong with you to what's strong with you shifted my thoughts from being clouded with negativity to being illuminated by ideas of success and the fire of inner courage. Great advertising makes you think and feel, and this campaign did exactly that for me.

What's Strong with You?!

What are your strengths? Think, journal, and spend time with your strengths because how you think about your strengths will help you leverage them. List them out. Go deep.

Give intentional thought to how each of your strengths accelerated your achievements and provide examples. Think about the strengths you can lean on when you are not at your best that may help you show up stronger.

When you know your strengths, you can intentionally leverage them to gain more power and confidence each day.

We are so hard on ourselves. We see our weaknesses clearly. When something goes wrong, our irrational inner critic speaks in harsh tones and passes merciless judgments.

Does any of this sound familiar?

Lost car keys: *What's wrong with me?*

Typo in your email: *I'm so careless.*

Forgotten calendar appointment: *I'm such a loser.*

Not speaking up in a meeting: *I'm so bad at this. I just can't.*

Calling someone you've met ten times by the wrong name: *I suck.*

Replying all on an email when what you wrote was for just one colleague: *I'm so stupid, just the worst person ever! What's wrong with me?*

Focusing on your strengths creates less drama.

Once you know your strengths, you can intentionally aim them at your success. If you are having trouble clarifying your strengths, ask a friend, family member, or colleague. Read testimonials from your clients. Look at performance reviews for the good stuff. Look at the recommendations people have written on your behalf.

What if you woke up each morning and asked: What's Strong with Me?

High achievers focus on their strengths and use them to counter-balance their weaknesses. That's an example of being intentional. You don't have to be good at everything. Be good at what you are good at and what comes naturally.

You will experience faster growth for yourself with your strengths over prioritizing improving on your weaknesses.

When you apply your strengths, real change takes hold.

Think about what's strong with you. Use this worksheet to help you explore your strengths, go to:

christinalangdon.com/success

Self-Doubt: What I Know for Sure

A few years ago, I was once introduced as an expert in emotional intelligence, and I cringed upon hearing it. Negative thoughts started spinning in my head, and I began questioning my capabilities.

What do I know for sure? I have thirty years of sales and marketing experience. For almost twenty of those years, I worked for Martha Stewart Living Omnimedia where I helped launch 23 new media brands. I've held the Chief Revenue title at the media innovation brand, Fast Company. I am certified in both leadership coaching and emotional intelligence. I've started two companies and bought a third, and ran them profitably. I survived a divorce. I raised three incredible children. I survived a divorce. These are facts.

Am I an expert in any of it? What I know for sure is that I'm an expert in myself. That expertise is what sets me apart. There is no one quite like me. No letters after my name, certifications, or diplomas will make me more of an expert in me. It's who I am, and it's what sets me apart.

You are also unique, which distinguishes you from others.

Self-doubt touches all of us at some point. For some of us, it happens more often than we'd like. It erodes our confidence and tugs at our ability to perform at our best.

Emotional intelligence experts define self-regard as the ability and tendency to both like and have confidence in yourself while considering both positive and negative qualities.

When self-doubt creeps up, I lay a comforting hand on my heart and remind myself what I would tell a close friend. I am not perfect, but one of a kind.

SNEAKY SECRETS

The Sneaky Secret of I Don't Know

I don't know.

Does this sound familiar, What if I don't make the right decision? I don't want to make the wrong decision. I know I should. What will people think of me? What if I fail? I just don't know.

These negative discovery questions are unproductive thoughts and don't get you closer to a decision.

You want to make the right decision, not the wrong one. But what does right or wrong even mean? Start there. Are you holding yourself in judgment? That's not a great place to make any decision from.

According to the research of Dr. Fred Luskin of Stanford University, a human being has approximately 60,000 thoughts per day—90% of these are repetitive.

Most decisions we ponder have already been made in our subconscious long before we consciously decide. For instance, when we get up from the table and walk, that's a decision. We make it subconsciously and then get up and do it. Or when we first learned how to put on a seat belt, we looked for where the belt is attached near the window, found the strap to pull down on, looked to find where to lock it in. Now, we do it without looking or consciously thinking about it. All are decisions that we are not thinking about consciously.

I went back and forth on a decision to invest in coaching certification. An endless circle of questions looped through my head. Could

I find the time? I worried about who I would be on the other side of it. While I knew I would grow, the uncertainty of not knowing exactly what would be different for me, made me fearful. I worried about the cost. Was this irresponsible of me? What would people think of me? What if I failed? Could I be successful? Would I measure up? Was this the right thing for me? The idea of it being the right decision was a big one for me. This is a thought that has held me back on many occasions. All of these battling thoughts depleted me of both time and energy.

Those thoughts were keeping me small. Subconsciously, I decided to say yes long before I recognized that I had. The battle in my head felt necessary before I could accept it. Time wasted and energy depleted.

When I listened to my intuition, my inner mentor, and the gnawing whispers, and stopped questioning myself, I let go of the negative thoughts and gave in. Entering my credit card was an easy first step to the extraordinary future I'm now working towards living.

Google defines decision-making as the cognitive process resulting in selecting a belief or a course of action among several possible alternative options.

Decision-making is a process. Be deliberate about your process. Remove judgment from it. Recognize the thoughts of fear. Look for the resistance and then ask why. Then allow yourself to make the decision.

Listen to your subconscious by writing down your thoughts about the decision. Journal, draw a mind map, and free write about the decision. Whatever works best for you. Putting the ideas to your questions on paper will present you with data and help you begin the more thoughtful process of listening to what you want. Commit to giving space to the decision—instead of the battle you think is necessary.

One question I find helpful is, "What will the decision mean to me today, next week, or five months from now?"

Listen for the 'buts' that are resistors, and write them down.

Resistance is often an avoidance strategy.

Maybe the struggle isn't with the decision but with what you're avoiding.

Once you've made this decision, get ahead of others before they become rushed, before the circle of questions. Proactive decision-making allows you to create what you want for yourself and your extraordinary life.

Take back the willy-nilly of decision crises. Don't wait to clear your plate to make that decision that will have you moving forward. Get ahead of the decisions that zap you, hold you back, keep you trapped in the judgment of yourself, and make you feel like you can't make a decision.

This is living your extraordinary life more consciously.

The Sneaky Secret of Recognition

There's a sneaky secret behind a desire for recognition.

We all love hearing how great we are.

That's being human.

Here's what's sneaky. When you use validation as a measure of your self-worth, you'll never measure up.

The need for recognition shows up in things like:

• Checking emails way after hours, and immediately responding.
• Saying YES to every meeting, even when you don't need to be there.
• Leaving your calendar open for anyone to book time for what works for them not you.

Perhaps you worry what people will think if you don't answer right away or what they will say about you if you don't show up.

Maybe you worry how it will reflect on your leadership.

You want to be liked, so you people please, which is another sneaky way you look for recognition.

I was on that same hamster wheel for years, always hungry to be recognized and liked. It was exhausting to think that my identity was only as strong as how well-liked I was and the frequency of praise for my work.

I wanted to sell more than anyone. I wanted the commissions. But I also wanted recognition. And just like the commissions, when I received recognition, I wanted it again next year—an insidious, never-ending need.

I learned how to let go.

It starts by making decisions from what you want for yourself, not the story that loops in your head making up thoughts about what people will think about you.

Deciding for yourself ahead of time and not bending to the expectations of others is powerful.

That's self-validation. This is a path to worrying less and increasing your confidence.

Self-validation is a learned skill. It frees you from the need to hear how great you are from anyone but yourself.

Here's a three-step process:

Step 1: Acceptance

According to Psychology Today, self-validation is the act of accepting your own internal experience, including your thoughts and feelings.

Acceptance is the key word. Accepting yourself is an earned skill that can be a real superpower. Accepting yourself means having compassion for who you are at this very moment. Compassion for both the good and the not-so-good; it's ok to be who you are in the moment. Here's a thought that might help you understand further: I am what I am today. I will learn from it to become who I want to be.

There will be days when you fall short, as we all do. Use those times as data to learn from. Don't weaponize those experiences against yourself.

Falling short has nothing to do with your intrinsic self-worth. A bad moment is not a reason to shame or blame yourself. When you shame yourself, it strikes at your self-worth. Become aware. Decide instead to have compassion for yourself. This is the antidote for shame.

With self-compassion you self-validate.

In her book, *Atlas of the Heart*, Brene Brown recommends taking Dr. Kristin Ness' Self-Compassion test, self-compassion.org/self-compassion-test/.

Give it a go, and see how self-compassionate you are, or not.

Step 2: Examine Earned Experience

You may struggle with believing in yourself or what you're capable of. Most people do.

It becomes easier when you know that what you can achieve is built on what you've already achieved.

Dig deep into your accomplishments, both professional and personal. This is the culmination of who you are today and the foundation for future success. Making a list of evidence of your success is one of the easiest and most effective validation tools.

It's where belief takes hold and is nurtured, and your self-worth grows along with it.

This is an exercise that people resist doing because they believe they already know their accomplishments. When written out in great detail, it becomes a full story not just pieces of memory.

View your success through the lens of what you've already created and use the energy it creates to create more success.

Step 3: Prioritize

Self-validation relies on putting on your oxygen mask before attempting to help others.

Want to know the funny thing about prioritizing yourself? You'll end up pleasing more people and showing up with more impact. Prioritizing yourself has a multiplier effect that has you showing up more effectively with others. When people see you happier, they are happier which is a pretty powerful strategic byproduct.

Accepting that you are enough just the way you is pure self-validation.

Coming from that place of certainty feels so much better than asking, Am I enough?

And, enough with the word enough!

Let me use it one final time. When will you decide that you've had enough of seeking validation from others?

You are one of a kind. No validation needed.

The Sneaky Secret of Success

Success.

How do you define it?

A client reached out a year after we had worked together. I asked what her long-term success looked like; she laughed and replied that I always ask the most challenging questions.

We spend a lot of time in our hard work towards success but not enough time defining what it would look like when we've arrived.

Success is not defined by a job title or money in the bank. Job titles are an acknowledgment of success and achievement and financial rewards are the result of success. If you define success by money, how much money would define success? Most people who make a dollar then want to make $10, then $100, and so on. Money is not a measuring stick to success.

How will you know when you have reached success?

I define success as leading from my vision and making an impact every day.

My vision is to bring joy and ease to ambitious high-achievers who want to create a massive impact and leave a mark. My vision has me changing people's lives for the better and leaving a legacy with my words. My vision comes from feeling empowered, decided, and in service. My vision also has me creating all of this on my terms.

When I'm leading from my vision, I believe it will produce the success I want.

Years ago, I defined success through my title, sales numbers, the people I met (Cher!), and the travel that accompanied my role. I used words to define success from need instead of how I wanted to feel—empowered, effective, impactful, and passionate.

I wasn't necessarily wrong, but I was unclear.

Unclear about how I wanted to feel about success.

Unclear about what impact I wanted to have.

Unclear that money and titles would not bring me happiness.

However, thoughtfully connecting where happiness and success intersect starts with intentionally mapping it.

Commit it to paper and rewrite it frequently—this is not optional—as you'll experience detours and speed bumps along the way that will require a rethink.

Success is in the journey. Like any journey, you'll need a clear roadmap. The straightest path to success comes from a devotion to it. Success is the result of discipline and consistency.

With discipline, you don't have to think about what you're doing. You just do it. Doing creates efficiencies accelerating you closer to your vision, and, ultimately, your extraordinary life.

After you've committed your vision for success in writing, enter it into your calendar. Actualize your vision and roadmap for success by prioritizing it in your calendar. Decide how many hours each week you will dedicate to working on achieving those things you know will get you one step or one week closer to your success. Map out milestones in your calendar to bring accountability to you. These things alone give you permission to focus on your future instead of the busy of the day.

Then, decide on milestones to remind you of how far you've come and to celebrate your progress. We do not acknowledge or praise ourselves enough. That's discipline, and your vision begins unfolding when it is committed to the calendar.

The Sneaky Secret of Broken Promises

What would you say if I asked how often you broke a promise to your son or daughter?

What about breaking a promise to your sister, mom, or husband?

I'm not talking about breaking a promise due to something significant like an emergency. I mean breaking a promise because something more important came up.

Rarely, if ever, am I right? You rarely break promises to the people you love.

Then why do you break promises to yourself?

Promises can be as simple as eating less, exercising more, or showing up on time to meetings. Bigger promises might include lowering your stress, going for that dream job, committing to not losing your temper, or getting rid of that toxic person on your team.

Are you not important?

Are you any less important?

Breaking promises to yourself is a double whammy.

Every time you break a promise to yourself, you are one more step behind in achieving something you desire.

Breaking promises to yourself keeps you from something you want with negative consequences to you.

And, with each broken promise, it gets easier to break another one, and another one, leading to a breaking promises cycle.

That's the first whammy.

The second whammy is all the thoughts of blame and self-recrimination that surface as a result.

You 'should' all over yourself.

Said another way...

You sh#t on yourself.

I should have! Would have! Could have!

Should-ing sits with blame. You blame yourself for not following through, getting distracted, or letting things derail you.

But when you don't show up for yourself and your goals—like that promise to stand up for yourself in a meeting, ask for a raise, or fire that employee—that irrational inner critic runs amok, creating negative drama that plays on repeat in your head.

It zaps you of your energy. Breaking promises to yourself almost always drains more energy from you than keeping that promise.

Should-ing also impacts your self-esteem.

That's the double whammy.

What if putting yourself first is keeping promises to others?

When you fulfill a personal promise, you show up better for the people in your life.

When you are happy, accomplished, and good about keeping your promises to yourself, the people you love will see how happy you are.

And, they'll see who they can become.

You are their role model.

Do you want the most important people in your life to break their promises to themselves? Of course not.

Do you want them not to achieve because they don't prioritize themselves? Of course, you don't.

If you don't want that for them, show them how it's done.

Choose courage over should-ing.

Start doing what you've promised yourself to start living your extraordinary life.

LEADING

Death by Calendar

Do you ever think I'm tired of managing it all.

The demands for my time are out of control.

I'm more accountable to my calendar than I am myself.

I want to do all these things but have no time.

I'm booked out for weeks.

You may think this is because of a runaway calendar.

But that's just a lie you tell yourself.

In truth, it's a reflection of a runaway mind.

When your mind is cluttered, messy, and full of drama, it shows up in how you spend your time.

That's why I say your calendar reflects your mind, not the other way around.

You might think, "I'm in back-to-back meetings that have to happen, and when I'm not in meetings, I've got sh*t to do!"

When you say 'yes' to something, you say 'no' to something else.

When the mind is messy, it looks at everything the same. If it's all important, is anything important? If everything is a 'yes' then there are no 'no's.' That's the messy mind at work.

Your mind will start blaming it on circumstances—which are often outside of your control—but a circumstance doesn't create the thoughts that say you can never get anything done! You cannot change a circumstance, but you can change how you think about managing your time.

Your calendar reflects your priorities and future; if it doesn't, that's on you.

Your calendar can be a crutch or a foundational tool for mindfully crafting your future.

Some people use their calendars as an organizing system and put today's calendar before the future of the business. It's how I used to work.

You are the owner of your time. Show up by design, not simply by default due to your calendar.

I'm sure you've heard the following in some version,

"How you show up for anything is how you show up for everything," is a powerful quote from Martha Beck, author and life coach, I often think about in all aspects of my life from business, goals, and my relationships.

If you want to create the time to make your future, here's an exercise that my clients find both enlightening and empowering.

A Calendar Audit

Owning your calendar begins with understanding where you are currently spending your time and then deciding how you want to spend your time in the future.

1. Create 'time buckets' for different types of activity, and color code each one (meetings, networking, client service, finance, marketing, bookkeeping, partnerships, product development), and don't forget to add your exercise and meeting prep time. Color coding will help you quickly recognize the kind of day/ week ahead of you at a glance. I use green for planning and blue for low-value work.

2. Examine and analyze where you are spending your time. Look for your time leaks of low-value and low-impact work and the amount of time you spend on that work. Go back one to two months and move your time into the color-coded buckets. From these weeks of color-coded time, you'll begin to see patterns emerge. Average it out into one week and call it My Current Time Spent.

After doing this, clients tell me that they knew they were spending time doing low-value work and didn't realize how much time they spent each week on work with little long-term impact or the amount of time on work that was simply distractions.

To see how you value your time, come up with your hourly rate—based on the revenue you want to make this year or your salary divided by 1,920 hours-(a 40-hour work week multiplied by 48 weeks taking holiday and vacation weeks into consideration) then multiply it by the number of hours you spent on low-value work.

Was that hour of admin work worth your hourly rate? Would that time be better spent by someone on your team or your Virtual Assistant (VA) with a lower hourly rate? Every hour you spend on admin or low-value work that can be delegated costs the business money, time, and, therefore, your future. That is not an overstatement after you've done the math.

3. Now, take back your time. Using the same color-coding system, map out the calendar you want and call it My Future. What would your ideal calendar look like, with dedicated time for working 'on' your business versus working 'in' your business?

You get to decide when this future calendar will be achievable. Will it be three weeks or three months from now? Begin by calendaring the must-haves: exercise, planning, strategizing, and super-thinking time.

Here is where the C.E.O. mind kicks in. Determine what you want to do and what is best for the business' long-term future, and be ruthless about what you can outsource to reclaim your time. This is the time you need to create your future.

With the remaining time, you will want to prioritize what you'll do with it based on high-value/high-impact work. Now, this is where belt-tightening comes into play. If you spend ten hours a week on low-value activities and want to reduce it to one hour, do it. From that decision, evaluate the steps needed to make it happen. It could mean hiring a virtual assistant—which has been life-changing for me—or delegating in another way. Awareness is a powerful thing, and with it, planning gets easier.

Seeing these two calendars will empower you to think differently about what you want and what needs to happen for your time to be more impactful.

4. Look forward to next week and the week after. Call it My WIP Calendar. What can you change today about how you want to spend your time? This is your work-in-progress calendar that looks different from your current calendar and looks closer to your future calendar. Each week, continue to work on owning your time to achieve the future calendar that will have you working on more high-value work with a higher degree of happiness.

Stop leaving your calendar up to chance and allowing someone else to book your time without your permission. If they have, take the time back.

This exercise will reduce the time you spend wrestling with an out-of-control calendar.

When you prioritize your time, you will start to show up with more clarity and control over your most valuable asset—your time.

User Manuals are Not Only for Cars and Appliances

A C-suite executive starting a new role once asked for my support in making a good first impression. I asked her to describe her user manual, and she looked at me quizzically.

On my first day at Fast Company, I was ushered into the conference room to meet my team. It was a team that had been without a leader for some time, and we were all a bit uneasy in that first meet and greet.

I shared that:

- I'm direct, sometimes to a fault.
- My values are rooted in family, exceptional service, passion, and hard work.
- I believe we should learn something new every day and go teach it to someone.
- Expect feedback, both good and bad, frequently.
- I like to overcommunicate and expect the same from my team.
- Mistakes can always be handled once responsibility is taken.
- Always overdeliver for your teammates and for your business.
- Know your facts, and deliver them without the fluff.
- I'm at my best when I'm thinking big and pushing boundaries.
- My biggest weakness is in planning ahead and the details.
- I'm a single mom (at the time) with three kids, and they are my first priority.

I wanted to set the stage. I wanted them to know me and not just what was in my LinkedIn profile, but the real stuff that was important to working together. Knowing how I operate; we'd quickly move beyond the relationship warm-up and get to work.

This was my user manual for my personal brand at work.

The concept of a user manual isn't mine. It originated in the New York Times 'Corner Office' column. It suggests that creating a user manual reduces anxiety and uncertainty, allowing people to get to business. It removes the process of trial and error and the awkward dance of learning how to work well with someone. With deep transparency, you save time and energy and boost productivity.

With your user manual, you can shorten the learning curve by removing many of the uncertainties of a new relationship and instead foster alignment, create understanding, reduce potential communication issues, establish preferences early, and minimize surprises.

Sharing your user manual will help people work better for you and with you, especially in the hybrid work environment.

I now recommend creating a user manual as an exercise for each team member. As a next step, have your team roll up their user manuals into one mutually agreed user manual for the team. Doing so will help establish the rules of engagement and connect team members deeper. The team user manual can also quickly identify when individuals, or the team, have veered off course.

Today, I would go a step further from my earliest user manual.

My list would now include:

- My values
- Communication preferences
- Leadership expectations
- When I'm at my best
- When I'm not at my best
- My strengths
- My weaknesses
- Where I can use the most help
- Which activities give me energy
- Which activities do not give me energy
- What I don't have patience for
- How I handle conflict
- How to help me
- What people misunderstand about me

Since none of us are alike, why do we try to work with everyone in the same way? The better a team knows one another, the easier it will be to navigate conflict, empathize with one another, and support each other when sharing and fostering new ideas.

Leading is Not Telling

In my last corporate role, I repeatedly got into my car after nine-hour days of asks, requests, questions, and so many decisions. I had no energy left, not even enough to make the simple decision to turn on the radio, let alone decide on the station.

This was one indication of burnout.

Decision fatigue is real. According to Wikipedia, it refers to the deteriorating quality of decisions made by an individual after a long session of decision-making.

In leadership, people ask you to weigh in all day long. Partly because they need direction and value your opinion and because most desire to be led.

Whatever your signature brand of leadership is, consider mitigating decision fatigue by leading from a coaching mindset.

Leading from a coaching mindset is rooted in, what I call, the Language of Leadership. It's rooted in curiosity and driven by powerful questioning.

Like most leaders, your brain is wired to answer questions, solve problems, and fix issues. But as you rise to lead more powerfully, pay close attention to how much you are deciding, fixing, and telling versus actually leading.

Leadership is not telling.

Telling doesn't provide a new perspective.

Telling isn't teaching.

Telling doesn't shift perspective.

Telling isn't creating a learning experience.

Telling doesn't allow them to think harder and deeper.

Telling doesn't guarantee that someone is hearing or understanding. Telling someone what you know does no good if they don't understand. Read back that sentence again.

If they don't understand what you are telling them, then what you are telling them may as well be falling on deaf ears. As a result, work won't get done or done right, and you'll only become more frustrated.

Leading with a coaching mindset is about asking questions to ensure people understand you, the project at hand, and what success looks like.

Leading with a coaching mindset trains people to think for themselves. They not only learn more, but they'll also build more belief in themselves. When we believe in ourselves, we show up in the world very differently.

Leading with a coaching mindset is about their growth and yours.

You may be thinking that you don't have time for it, but here's the thing, when you help people grow, they will make more decisions for you, and you'll reclaim more time for yourself.

If you get stuck in the perfectionist's trap of doing everything for yourself, consider that there is always more than one way to do something. Though, you know that already!

You may also be saying that it's easier for you to do it; then you might be in a vicious cycle that is suffocating your leadership and ability to scale your business.

Leading with a coaching mindset is rooted in getting curious with powerful questions like these:

• What do you need to know?
• What have you already tried?
• What is your thought process?
• What else have you considered?
• What would make our conversation most helpful?
• What does your gut say?
• What does success look like here?
• What outcome do you want?
• What will you do if you get stuck?

And, What else?

I've found that the first response to a question isn't what's at the heart of an issue. Taking a conversation deeper can be achieved by following up your first question with, What else?

What comes after powerful questioning? Listening.

When I was getting my coaching certification, my coach recommended something. I was to take a sticky note, write four letters on it, and then stick it on my desk or computer so that it was always in sight.

W.A.I.T.

That stands for: Why Am I Talking?

Think about how much time you spend talking versus your colleagues.

Listening is one of the most powerful coaching tools, and it is equally powerful when leading. Listen to not only what is said but also what's behind it. And then ask, What else?

I work on my listening skills every day. I use all sorts of tips and tricks, including looking for the color of people's eyes—yes, even on a Zoom call—because if I know their eye color, I know I'm present and focused on them.

People rise to the expectations others set for them.

Stop telling.

Set expectations.

Get curious.

Listen.

Guide others to make powerful decisions for you.

Your Words Matter

Words are the building blocks of our thoughts. Positive thoughts generate feelings and actions that create our desired results, and negativity creates less-than-desirable results. Words have the energy, power, and ability to help, hurt, lift, or squash us.

Just.

Just needs to be eliminated from your vocabulary. It minimizes everything that comes after it. It marginalizes what you are saying.

But.

But negates anything that you've thought, said, or written before it. Your priorities, preferences, and defensiveness show up after 'but.' Choose a better transition word.

Help me understand.

Instead of sharing disappointment or responding punitively when something doesn't go as planned, pause and say, 'Help me understand.'

Those three words give you time to gather your thoughts while helping you gain understanding and steer the other person into ownership. In doing so, you may learn something you didn't know.

What can I count on you for?

Enrolling people into your goals or mission takes consistent communication and collaboration. When you ask for a commitment, there is an opportunity for buy-in and acknowledgment. It's far more effective than saying 'I need...' or 'You need to...'.

Again, telling is not leadership.

Choosing your words is the key to leading yourself to lead others and writing your life script to create an extraordinary life.

Better Decision-Making

Decision-making is integral to success.

Here's a simple rule: Don't make a permanent decision based on a temporary emotion.

Making decisions from a place of emotional drama will bring more drama.

A client shared with me the misalignment of expectations and effort she was experiencing with her co-founder. It was causing a massive fissure in their business partnership that was seeping into their personal relationship and negatively hitting the business' bottom line.

By her account, it was showing up with a lot of drama, leaving her feeling disappointment, frustration, and insecurity.

Drama has a snowball effect.

It gains momentum until you recognize it for what it is.

I asked my client to look at what she wanted from a 30,000-foot view. To think about the outcomes she wanted to create from their upcoming strategic planning meeting together. This prompt pulled her out of the headspace of drama and into one of curiosity, ideation, possibility, and clarity for the business.

From there, she could see that throwing down the snowball of emotions would be messy and full of emotion for both her and her co-founder. Negative emotions were not on the list of outcomes she wanted.

Instead of coming from a place of being right or from hurt feelings, she got curious. She honed in on her vision for the meeting and worked backward to compose a list of questions for their strategic planning meeting.

She recognized the potential to double, and even triple, revenue with a realigned and reinforced partnership.

She decided to focus on the future—and bold outcomes—rather than the current, distracting drama.

Much better feelings resulted from that thought exercise. Clean thoughts.

Football legend Tom Brady's decision to retire (the first time) is a teachable lesson in using emotional intelligence (EQ) to manage internal drama while managing that of others. In his post-game press conference, Tom shared that he wouldn't make a permanent decision based on the emotions he was feeling right after losing his last game of the season. This statement is a masterclass in EQ from the GOAT (Greatest Of All Time).

To make decisions from the outcomes you want, start by asking:
• What do I know about either side of the decision?
• What do I need to know before I make the decision?
• What are the facts versus the story (what could be proven in a court of law)?
• What would be a wrong decision?
• What is my definition of the right decision?
• What do I need to feel to believe in the decision?

- What steps will I take if I make the wrong decision?
- Who needs to be considered?

Keep in mind that a wrong decision gives you data to make better decisions in the future.

Don't make decisions from scarcity or hustle-based mindsets. 'Hustle and grind' decisions come from a place of need versus want. Neediness grabs at scarcity. Wanting is where creation begins.

Get out of the headspace created by drama. Instead, use the data for awareness and clarity to help make decisions that will fuel your extraordinary life.

Go the Extra Mile. It's Never Crowded

I worked for Martha Stewart Living Omnimedia for almost twenty years, leading sales and marketing. With ID badge #9, I was one of her first full-time employees. In the early days, as she was gaining global recognition for elevating home keeping to an art form, Martha was often questioned by her critics around the origination of her recipes and ideas, and if they were hers alone.

Walmart is launching Walmart+, which is Amazon Prime by another name. Tesla was not the first electric car manufacturer, but Tesla's brand value sets it apart. Walmart and Tesla are both trailblazers despite not being the first to offer what they offer.

The rarity of real innovation has businesses striving to uncover new value from what already exists.

Martha's carrot cake was unique not for its ingredients, ratios, or mixtures but for its presentation and point of view; the world is better with a delicious and beautifully appointed cake.

I believe that point of view is the currency of innovation today.

Innovation is a huge word that can overwhelm and seem out of reach. What about taking the enormity of innovation and thinking of it in terms of value? Walmart+ when launched will be very similar to Amazon Prime, bringing new value to its millions of brand-loyal customers.

What value can you create to offer a slight edge to you, your business, or your career? What makes your point of view more persuasive? Enough to be memorable, get asked back, and even stop them in their tracks.

A client of mine was the C.E.O. of an accounting company and wanted to explore how his firm could be innovative. We discussed what exceptional value and point of view his firm could bring that would be distinguishing and even disruptive. We talked about his exceptional team members and their laser focus on client service.

Filing my taxes is like having my teeth cleaned. Never fun, but it must be done. What if my accountant was someone I enjoyed learning from and hearing their point of view because they always bring new context and a growth mindset? Dare I say they care about me and my business?

Teaching me something new with each interaction in pursuit of making me and my business better; or making the process of filing my taxes feel more like a learning, growth, and strategic experience and less like a teeth cleaning.

Our discussion would play an instrumental role in next year's business and taxes.

The C.E.O.'s vision now comes from how he wants each client to feel when they working with the company. To that end, he has invested in each of his employees getting personal coaching and created new policies including allowing additional non-billable hours for client development to help them build stronger client relations. Employee turnover has decreased. Employee engagement has increased along with the number of clients the firm is servicing.

Why not break the rules of history and the patterns of 'That's not how we do it here.' You don't need to be the first in the arena to make something new or innovative.

At Martha Stewart Living Omnimedia, I remember getting a request for a proposal for a media plan from a gift company that had filed for bankruptcy. I struggled to understand how a few fourth-quarter advertising pages could lift any company out of bankruptcy. Had we sent our go-to proposal, it would have been what they were expecting; instead, we presented a concept for creating a Martha Stewart curated gift product that would be on the front page of the gift company's holiday catalog as the centerpiece for the gift company's holiday sales and the star of their advertising. Our view was to think bigger and go beyond the expected. Martha Stewart Living Omnimedia took the lion's share of the client's entire fourth-quarter budget. The byproduct of going the extra mile had a multiplier effect on their business and ours.

Average is over. Go the extra mile. Do the unexpected. Innovation comes from delivering unexpected value.

I give a lot of my content away, make it public, and offer it to other coaches in my networks. I want to deliver exceptional value in every exchange including with those I work with and those I don't. I've been asked if I am worried my work would be copied or repurposed. I believe my process of engagement, my approach, and my point of view sets my business apart. I'm an expert only in me. That's the secret to my slight edge.

"Go the extra mile. It is never crowded."

–Mel Robbins

Bob Goff, bestselling author, whose most recent book *Dream Big: Know What You Want, Why You Want It, and What You're Going to Do About It*, puts his cell phone number in the back of his books. Even after selling over 2 million books, he invites readers to call him. And he answers. This is one of the many elements that sets Bob and his brand apart. This is his unique point of view (UPOV).

You can be sure his editor told him not to do that and shared the downside of such a decision. This is Bob's innovation.

Bob believes people feel great on the other side of the line when he personally answers the phone and says 'hello.'

Controlling how, when, and where you show up can be your direct line to innovation. This is your UPOV. Bob says he wants to leave a legacy of availability. I think that's innovative. That's Bob's thing, and it may not be yours.

How are you wired for innovation? Try something out. Take a chance. If it doesn't yield results, try something else.

I love Bob's innovation for printing his phone number in his book so much that I want to offer mine here: 917-359-4725. I am looking forward to hearing from you.

The Secret to Your Slight Edge

You know that person who, when they walk in the room, you feel their energy?

That person who, when they present, have you at hello?

That person who, when their email hits your inbox, you open it with anticipation, expectation, and curiosity that it will deliver something intelligent, insightful, and witty?

They leave a mark every time. They stand out.

As the future of business evolves, how are you growing your personal and professional brand to keep up? No matter your profession, the secret to your slight edge means defining and knowing your brand and your brand value to leave a mark every time.

Jeff Bezos famously said, "Your brand is what other people say about you when you're not in the room."

You are a brand. The Brand of You, like any other brand, requires consideration, planning, and execution. The Brand of You is doing the work to ensure your brand is represented in and throughout everything you do. Decide ahead of time what you want to be known for as a brand. The impact you want to make in your industry, with your team, and for your clients ensures they know exactly what you stand for, who you are, and what they can expect from you with each and every interaction. Fast Company called it the C.E.O. of Me Inc.

And today—more than ever in this virtual and hybrid world—your brand is your most valuable asset to help you stand out.

According to Seth Godin, entrepreneur, author, and speaker, *"a brand is the set of expectations, memories, stories, and relationships that, taken together, account for a consumer's decision to choose one product or service [or person] over another."*

The Brand of You is defined by:

• Expectations you set and over deliver.
• Memories you create that are positive, rich, and valuable.
• Stories you tell that are remembered.
• Relationships you build that are deep and trusted.

In our highly competitive world, that is only becoming more so under the pressure of hybrid work, you must distinguish yourself from all the other brilliant people. The Secret to Your Slight Edge requires it to be prescriptive in order to be truly exceptional.

This is about genuine authenticity. This is not about doing something for show or a 'fake it to make it' situation. It's your signature. A signature that when left, is a reminder of you. It's not made up; it makes you, you.

Developing your brand requires a relentless focus on how you add value, what you're proud of, and, most importantly, what you can shamelessly take credit for achieving.

Begin by identifying the qualities or characteristics that make you distinctive. Ask yourself, 'What do I do/what can I do that adds/that can add remarkable, measurable, distinguished, and distinctive value?' Developing your brand has you playing on offense versus defense.

Forget the job description and focus on what you uniquely bring to your job, customers, and industry. Delivering is expected. Expected is average. Average is over.

So, ask yourself,

What do I do that I am most proud of?

What have I accomplished that I can unabashedly brag about?

When I go the extra mile, I _____.

Here's the tough part: you must do it daily. When you know your brand value, it manifests in everything you do. The Secret to Your Slight Edge needs to be written down and clearly articulated as a reminder that you can call on when you veer off the path or hit a confidence power outage. It's a personal measuring stick for personal success.

Ideally, it will take the form of two sentences that, when reading aloud, so closely represents you that anyone who knows you will instinctively know those sentences describe you and only you.

You are distinctive. You are extraordinary. You bring value. Your value currency is your brand, as Jeff Bezos notably said. When you are not in the room, you'll have a pretty good idea about what people will say about you.

Take this work deeper with the Brand of You worksheet, which can be downloaded at:

christinalangdon.com/success

LAUNCHING

Game Changers Are Life Changers

We all have the same amount of time each day. What if you used your time in a way that doubled your impact?

Double the trouble. Double the fun, right?

I used to say this about my twin boys when they were toddlers. But what if you were to:

Double the Focus

Double the Impact

If you were to look at your goals, what is the one thing or one goal that, if you invested in it, would generate significantly more results for you?

That one thing, that would create a multiplier effect and give you back so much more than you put in?

That one thing that would deliver compounding results?

The one thing that if you double-downed on, would yield returns that would free you up for more growth?

Doubling-down is a phrase most often associated with blackjack. Let me be clear, I'm not asking you to gamble with your future. Instead, I'm asking you to bet on yourself. I'm asking you to believe in yourself and your ability to create massive success.

You can get to 10 by counting sequentially, 1, 2, 3, 4, 5, 6, 7, 8, 9, but you get to ten much faster if you multiply 2 x 5.

Dan Sullivan, coach and author, shares a concept that he refers to as 10x is easier than 2x. A link to his talk can be found on the resource page as well as here: youtube.com/watch?v=VEzLCU-oDvE

What's your multiplier?

Answering this is your GAME CHANGER.

Game changers are what you focus on today
to make you more successful tomorrow.

One of my clients double-downed on risk-taking as her game changer. She committed to taking one considerable risk every day in pursuit of launching her new company, so she filled a jar with M&Ms and permitted herself to eat one M&M every time she took a risk. Those risks included cold calls she didn't want to make and an investment she didn't have to spend on Facebook ads.

I recently asked her about the M&Ms. She said she'd stopped her creative incentive program. She no longer wanted the extra calories, but that risk-taking was now part of her routine. Risk-taking became normalized. And what was the result of her game changer? A few months after taking risks as a daily practice, her revenue grew exponentially; she hit her first six-figure quarter and consistently doubled that in quarters ever since.

When you double down in blackjack, you double the initial bet due to your confidence in your cards and/or your perceived weakness of the dealer's cards.

Double your bet to double your winnings. Deciding on your game changer is about discovering blind spots, clarifying your desires, and asking what's possible with 10x growth.

Ask yourself, 'What would be that one thing—area, skill, element, tactic—that would be the game changer for me, my career, or my business if I invested more time and energy into it?'

Let's look at a few to get the juices going:

• Strength (Risk taking)
• Weakness (Confidence)
• Product (service, workshop, research, sales, blog)
• Skill (Marketing)
• Process (Taking back your calendar)
• System (Customer Relationship Management or CRM)
• Business area (Sales)

Test your game changer by answering these questions.

If I committed time, resources, money, and effort:
• What incremental change will be produced?
• What does taking action toward my goals look like?
• What does full-on commitment look like?
• Will the added commitment become a multiplier?
  If the benefit doesn't have an impact in more than three places in your business, go back to the drawing board.
• Can the byproducts of your game changer be measured?
  If not, it's not your game changer.

And finally, does the inverse have an equally compounding negative effect?

For example, if confidence is your game changer, then the inverse is a continued lack of confidence with a cascading negative impact. If marketing is your Achilles' heel, then the inverse would be a lack of exposure, a weakened sales funnel, and/or stagnant or declining sales.

The Motivation Equation

Some think motivation is a flip of a light switch or a turn of an ignition key. That's not how it works. It isn't something that turns on and off.

I commonly hear from business leaders that they've lost their motivation. This trickles down to their teams. They share a lack of motivation leading to an absence of energy and engagement from their teams.

We all struggle with motivation. Imagine how much wasted time, money, and headaches business leaders would avoid if their teams were full of self-motivated workers.

Motivation comes from the Latin word to move. A derivative of that word is motive.

Instead of looking to quickly flip the switch to motivation, what if you looked for the ingredients? When I looked at my ingredients for my motivation, I found that it was comprised of ambition and action.

Ambition + Action = Motivation

People often don't like the word ambition. It suggests we are full of ourselves or pushing people aside for our gain. Instead, consider that we all want our lives to be better. To lose a few pounds. Be a more present parent. Drive more sales. Grow our businesses. Lead more effectively. We desire a new place of being. That wish or desire is ambition by another name. Our ambitions are an ingredient for motivation, no matter how big or small.

Next, get clarity on the actions needed to serve the ambition. Action plans sound daunting, but a drive without a destination makes for a long and uncertain route.

Take my Sunday Sunshine newsletter as an example. I had a desire that gnawed at me for a very long time. I had the ambition to share my thoughts and insights to help others achieve their highest potential. I wanted to share my thoughts and insights about what moves me and my passions. I had ambition, but ambition without action is simply thoughts gone unmet. I wasn't taking action required to invest in automation, build my database, and quiet my inner critic.

When I finally sent my first Sunday Sunshine in 2020, my motivation skyrocketed. I now look forward to writing each week. I hope my readers enjoy reading each Sunday as much as I love writing them. If you enjoy them, please feel free to share them with someone who could benefit! If you are not yet a reader, sign up with this link:

christinalangdon.com/subscribe

What we focus our attention on is what we prioritize. Are you prioritizing your motivation? Fulfilling our ambitions can feel scary. Taking action takes work. To achieve motivation means doing the hard work to prioritize your ambition every day and intentionally making it a part of your daily routine.

The truth is, there are no particular habits that make people successful. I believe everyone has the power within themselves to create long-lasting habits that motivate them to grow into who they were made to be. If you do not create long-lasting habits, your motivation may be in jeopardy.

Your payoff is the multiplier effect.

When your motivation is fired up, you create momentum. That momentum leads to more motivation.

Motivation + Daily Habit = Momentum

When you achieve momentum, you get into a flow—that most wonderful feeling you get when things are aligned and feel just right.

As I've said, the most influential person in your life is you. And when you recognize the influence that you have over yourself, it is a game changer.

I'm A Badass

I'm a Badass.

I love being called a Badass.

#badassbosslady is my Peloton user name.

@christinalangdonbosslady, my Instagram handle, is a riff on it as well.

Everyone has the potential to be a Badass.

Badasses work on how they show up for themselves, their teams, and organizations every day.

Badasses possess strength that they leverage for good.

Badasses create their world based on the outcomes they want.

The Badass in me sets a positive intention each day.

Being a Badass is not done at the expense of others, but in support of them.

Badasses extend trust to others.

Badasses motivate the Badass energy in others.

The Badass goes the extra mile—it's never crowded as per Mel Robbins quote earlier in this book.

Badasses take risks; it's what separates them.

Badasses have an abundance mindset which takes practice, discipline, and consistency.

Badasses remain disciplined, even if they don't feel like it.

Badasses are not born that way. Badasses decide how they want to show up and who they want to be. Badasses decide what they want to accomplish and do it daily which builds their Badass strength.

I didn't coin the concept of being a Badass. Many books and articles have been written about the term, but a powerful book got me charged up on the concept and my own badass self, *You Are a Badass: How to Stop Doubting Your Greatness and Start Living an Awesome Life* by Jen Sincero.

Who do you see as a Badass? What do you admire about them? Often the things you admire are the things you want for yourself.

Decide if you want to be a Badass.

What does it look like? How does it feel to be a Badass? What are your Badass characteristics?

My Badass characteristics include, but are not limited to, prepared, thoughtful, motivated, curious, energetic, passionate, in-service, gritty, and determined.

Badasses have the ability to become the best versions of themselves. They choose to create thoughts that create the feelings that put them into action and produce the desired results.

The foundation of how we Badasses show up as leaders comes from the positive thoughts we intentionally create about ourselves to produce extraordinary results.

The one question a Badass asks every day is,

———

What do I need to think is possible
in order to get the results I want today?

———

I answer this question every morning in order to lead myself in pursuit of my extraordinary life.

ACKNOWLEDGMENTS

This book was made possible by my family's deep support and unconditional love. The Sunday Sunshine newsletter is edited weekly by my incredible husband, Ron Potesky, who is always there to kindly tell me to go back and give it a rewrite. He always encourages my process, cheers me on, and lifts me up whenever I stumble. He initially inspired me to write this book. My business success has been made possible because Ron believed in me as I worked to believe in myself.

I also want to thank my children, Caroline, Jack, and Teddy, for their love and always helping when I ask, supporting my email open rates, and nudging me to publish this book. My stepsons, Charlie and Ben, are also on the support team. Ben gave me a much-needed kick in the pants to get this book done and has also been there throughout the process.

I am also blessed with my sister Michele who was a constant during my cancer treatment along with my close friend, Becky. I could not imagine where I would be today without the support I've received from these amazing, smart, talented, Badass women.

I also want to thank my clients who work hard pursuing and achieving extraordinary for themselves, their businesses, and their lives. They are my inspiration.

END NOTES

PREFACE
1. Christina Langdon, "Sunday Sunshine," christinalangdon.com, 2020-present, christinalangdon.com/subscribe

CHAPTER 1: BEGINNING

Are You a Dreamer or a Doer?
1. Your Extraordinary Future Worksheet, christinalangdon.com/success

CHAPTER 2: BECOMING

I Am
1. Daily Journal Prompts, christinalangdon.com/success

You're Invited to Create the Impossible
1. Possibility Formula Worksheet, christinalangdon.com/success

You Are Made for More
1. Rich Litvin, "11 Undervalued Superpowers," richlitvin.com/11-undervalued-superpowers/

Give Yourself an "A" Ahead of Time
1. Cameron, Julia. The Artist's Way, TarcherPerigee, revised edition 2002.
2. Sincero, Jen. You Are A Badass: How to Stop Doubting Your Greatness and Start Living an Awesome Life, Running Press Adult, 2013.

A Look Back to Move Forward
1. Robert Glazer, "Friday Forward," robertglazer.com/fridayfwd/
2. Robert Glazer, "Discovering and Developing Core Values, A Course from Robert Glazer," robertglazer.com/core-values-course/

Inspiration is the Holy Grail of Enthusiasm
1. Mautz, Scott. Find the Fire: Ignite Your Inspiration–and Make Work Exciting Again, HarperCollins, 2017.

Why Do Some People Achieve So Much and Others Don't?
1. Goff, Bob. Dream Big: Know What You Want, Why You Want It, and What You're Going to Do About It, Thomas Nelson Publishing, 2020.

A Life Full of Green Lights
1. McConaughey, Matthew. Greenlights, Crown, 2020.

CHAPTER 3: RESILIENCE

Detours & U-Turns
1. Cameron, Julia. The Artist's Way, TarcherPerigee, revised edition 2002.

Attitude is Everything
1. "What is Strong with You," YouTube.com, 2021, www.youtube.com/watch?v=2Zv42bXkgTo
2. Your Strengths & Gamechanger Worksheet, christinalangdon.com/success

CHAPTER 4: SNEAKY SECRETS

The Sneaky Secret of I Don't Know
1. Christine Comaford, "Got Inner Peace? 5 Ways To Get It NOW," Forbes, 2014, forbes.com/sites/christinecomaford/2012/04/04/got-inner-peace-5-ways-to-get-it-now

The Sneaky Secret of Recognition
1. Karyn Hall Ph.D., "Self-validation," Psychology Today, 2014, psychologytoday.com/us/blog/pieces-mind/201407/self-validation
2. Brown, Brene. Atlas of the Heart: Mapping Meaningful Connection and the Language of Human Experience, Penguin Random House, 2021.
3. Kristin Ness, Self-Compassion Test, self-compassion.org/self-compassion-test/

CHAPTER 5: LEADING

Death by Calendar
1. Martha Beck, "Making Time for Nothing," marthabeck.com, 2012, marthabeck.com/2012/02/making-time-for-nothing/

Leading is Not Telling
1. "Decision Fatigue," Wikipedia, en.wikipedia.org/wiki/Decision_fatigue

Go the Extra Mile. It is Never Crowded
1. "Go the extra mile. It is never crowded,", Motiveex, motiveex.com/quotes/mel-robbins-quotes/
2. Goff, Bob. Dream Big: Know What You Want, Why You Want It, and What You're Going to Do About It, Thomas Nelson Publishing, 2020.

The Secret to Your Slight Edge
1. Jeff Bezos, "Your brand is what other people say about you when you are not in the room," LinkedIn, 2020, www.linkedin.com/pulse/your-brand-what-people-say-you-when-room-jeff-bezos-anit-roy/
2. Tom Peters, "The Brand Called You," Fast Company, 1997, fastcompany.com/28905/brand-called-you
3. Seth Godin, "define: Brand," sethgodin.com, 2002, seths.blog/2009/12/define-brand/
4. Brand of YOU Worksheet, christinalangdon.com/success

CHAPTER 6: LAUNCHING

Game Changer are Life Changers
1. Dan Sullivan, "Future Thinking: 10X is Easier Than 2x," YouTube, 2017, youtube.com/watch?v=VEzLCU-oDvE
2. I'm a Bad Ass "Go the extra mile. It is never crowded," Motiveex, motiveex.com/quotes/mel-robbins-quotes/Sincero, Jen. You Are A Badass: How to Stop Doubting Your Greatness and Start Living an Awesome Life, Running Press Adult, 2013.

Take the Inspirations Beyond the Book

Get a boost for your week ahead with ideas, activities, and inspiration for intentionally creating your extraordinary future. Sign-up now to receive Sunshine Sunshine in your inbox at: christinalangdon.com/subscribe

For worksheets and additional content, go to:

christinalangdon.com/success

• Your Extraordinary Future Worksheet
• Daily Journal Prompts
• Possibility Formula Worksheet
• Your Strengths & Gamechanger Worksheet
• Brand of YOU Worksheet

ABOUT THE AUTHOR

Wendy Moynihan Photography

Christina Langdon is a passionate entrepreneur, speaker, and executive coach. After thirty years of leading sales and marketing teams at media brands, including Martha Stewart Living Omnimedia and Fast Company, she now helps leaders and businesses achieve more than they thought possible. She is known for building great brands and strengthening and sharpening teams and talent. She is a lifelong learner who welcomes a challenge. Christina makes big things happen for companies and people. Her mission is to help others achieve their 'extraordinary,' even when life gets in the way.

Christina earned her ACC from the International Coaching Federation and is certified in team and leadership coaching through Kick Start Your Edge. She is also certified in emotional intelligence training (EQi-2) through OKA. Her work has been featured in Thrive Global, Authority Magazine, Brit & Co, and Nasdaq.

Christina graduated from the University of Delaware with a degree in Communications. She lives in New Jersey with her husband—where they share five children and a successful home improvement business. Christina sits on the board of the Connie Dwyer Breast Cancer Foundation.

She is living her extraordinarily fulfilled life one day at a time.

christinalangdon.com | *christina@christinalangdon.com*

Made in the USA
Middletown, DE
15 July 2023

34992834R00086